THE U.S.S.R. IN IRAN

Also by FARAMARZ S. FATEMI:

Sufism: Message of Brotherhood, Harmony, and Hope (co-author)

Love, Beauty, and Harmony in Sufism (co-author)

THE U.S.S.R.
IN IRAN

The Background History of
Russian and Anglo-American
Conflict in Iran, Its
Effects on Iranian Nationalism,
and the Fall of the Shah

Faramarz S. Fatemi

SOUTH BRUNSWICK AND NEW YORK: A. S. BARNES AND COMPANY
LONDON: THOMAS YOSELOFF LTD

© 1980 by A. S. Barnes and Co., Inc.

A. S. Barnes and Co., Inc.
Cranbury, New Jersey 08512

Thomas Yoseloff Ltd
Magdalen House
136-148 Tooley Street
London SE1 2TT, England

Library of Congress Cataloging in Publication Data

Fatemi, Faramarz S
The U. S. S. R. in Iran.

    Bibliography: p.
    Includes index.
    1. Iran--Foreign relations--Russia. 2. Russia--
Foreign relations--Iran. 3. Iran--Politics and government--
1925-1979. I. Title.
DS274.2.R8F37   327.55047   80-23
ISBN 0-498-02532-2 (paperback)
ISBN 0-498-02340-0 (hardcover)

Printed in the United States of America

To my Mother and Father

Shayesteh *and* **Nasrollah**

Who gave me their love, guidance, and encouragement.

Contents

Preface

The overthrow and flight of the Shah of Iran, the seizure of the U. S. Embassy in Tehran by militants to gain the Shah's return and trial, and the consequent, continuing shock waves (including the Soviet invasion of Afghanistan) throughout the oil-rich Middle East all will be dealt with in the long run when one understands the historical background of the Iranian revolution. This book gives that perspective. Indeed, it was written over the last few years with a sense of the inevitability of its need, and of the inevitability of the Shah's downfall.

The reasons for the revolution were both internal and external, but it was the foreign interference that influenced the internal situation so adversely, leaving no other option but a revolt by the masses. The U.S.S.R.'s allies, from the Iranian communist party (the Tudeh) to their agents including the KGB, and the opposing Anglo-American interests, from the large international oil companies to the CIA, have a long history of involvement in Iran. This involvement extends at least as far back as 1907, the year of the first Anglo-Russian partition of Iran, and approximately the same time as the discovery of Iran's oil resources. It continues with: the establishment of the Pahlevi regime by the British in the 1920s; the second Anglo-Soviet partition in 1941 to stop growing German influence in the regime and region; the entrance of American interests during the first confrontation of the cold war to counter the Soviets' delayed withdrawal from Northern Iran (the presently troubled Azerbaijan area); the subsequent victory in 1946 of Iranian Prime Minister Ahmad Qavam in maneuvering the withdrawal of the Soviet Union (along with the first successful pressure brought by the newly-formed United Nations, apparently backed up by President Truman's military threats that at least implicitly included atomic war when the United States alone had the A-Bomb); the nationalization of the British oil fields by Prime Minister Mohammed Mussadeq in 1951, along with the first overthrow of the Shah in 1953; the role of the brothers Dulles, Kermit Roosevelt, and others in the temporary reversal of these nationalist victories; and finally this history concludes with a summary of the events of the Shah's second downfall, after having shown in detail how his overthrow was the unavoidable culmination of this long series of shocks by external forces to the body politic of Iranian nationalism.

This book is the first such undertaking that focuses on the key roles played by two Iranian leaders: Dr. Mohammed Mussadeq, who gave skilled and courageous leadership to the Fourteenth Majlis (Parliament) and Prime Minister Ahmad Qavam al-Saltaneh, who effectively put an end to the Soviet designs for achieving political/economic ascendency over the country.

Interviews were held with Dr. Ali Shayegan, minister of education in Qavam's cabinet; Nasser Khan Qasqai, the leader of the southern tribal uprising and the chief of the Qasqai tribes; Prince Mozaffar Firouz, deputy prime minister and minister of labor in Qavam's cabinet, who also headed the commission that negotiated with the Soviets and the Azerbaijan leadership, and Dr. Nasrollah S. Fatemi, former deputy of the Fourteenth Majlis and the co-sponsor of the Mussadeq resolution. Other interviews were held with a member of the central committee of the Tudeh party and a former representative of the Democratic party of Azerbaijan. For obvious reasons, and at their request, their names are not revealed.

I am grateful to them, for the opportunity of the interviews and their written statements, without which this work could have never been completed. I am also indebted to Professors

Saul K. Padover and the late Victor Baras of the Graduate Faculty, New School for Social Research, who were kind enough to read the manuscript and present to me their constructive suggestions.

F. M. Esfandiary has my special gratitude for his counsel, cooperation and helpful criticism. My appreciation to Sandra Asdoorian and Marian Johnson for their valuable assistance; and to Audrey March for her help in editing and with the index.

To my students, at Fairleigh Dickinson University, thank you for being a source of inspiration.

And finally, I am most grateful to my wife Afsar for her patience, assistance, and intellectualism.

Faramarz S. Fatemi
January 1980

THE U.S.S.R. IN IRAN

1 Anglo-Soviet Intervention, 1941

Reza Shah had been master of Iran for fourteen years at the outbreak of the Second World War, and had given the country strong nationalistic leadership.

He is said to have been born in 1878, in the Caspian Sea province of Mazanderan. Early accounts reveal a modest background—the lower strata of the military class—but later reports elevated the social standing of his family. It is not clear where he spent his youth, but some publications state that he joined the Cossack Brigade* in Tehran as a private at the age of fifteen.

Reza Khan's rise from trooper to throne was sudden, dramatic, and determined. He never received much formal education, but was daring, disciplined, and strong willed and

---

* The Persian Cossack Brigade, later a Division, was established following a request by Nasir ud-Din Shah in 1878, to the Russian Czar for help in developing a force modeled upon the Russian Cossacks. Staffed in part by Russian officers, it was the best trained force in the country. In due course many of the junior positions were filled by Iranians. The Russian officers of the Division resigned their commissions under British insistence in the autumn of 1920. An account of the information and early years of the Cossack Brigade, based on Russian sources, is given by Firuz Kazemzadeh in "The Persian Cossacks Brigade," *American Slavic and East European Review*, (Menasha, Wis., 1956), vol. 15, pp. 351-63.

had the politician's talent for opportunism. He attracted the attention of his Cossack superiors because of his unusual bravery, and within a short period attained the rank of Colonel.[1]

On 21 February 1921, Reza Khan, in collaboration with Seyyd Zia ud-Din Tabatabai, a pro-British editor of the newspaper *Raad*, utilized the services of the Cossacks to stage a *coup d'état* against the central government. Ahmad Shah appointed him commander of the Cossacks and *Sardar-i Sipah* "supreme military commander." Using the army effectively, Reza Khan maneuvered to become minister of war and later prime minister. He subsequently received dictatorial powers from the Fifth Majlis (Parliament).[2]

By 31 October 1925, the monarchy had weakened. With Ahmad Shah absent in Paris, and the British covertly encouraging his replacement with a strong leader as protection for their own interests, the Majlis brought about the dissolution of the Qajar dynasty.[3]

The Constituent Assembly met in Tehran on 12 December 1925, revising article 36 of the supplement to the constitution to read:

The Constitutional Monarchy of Iran is vested by the Constituent Assembly in His Imperial Majesty Reza Shah Pahlavi and his male descendants in succession.[4]

To free his country from British and Soviet influence, Reza Shah was willing to accept the friendship and support of any strong third power sufficiently distant so as not to endanger Iran's political independence—for example, France, the United States, or Germany. In fact, the latter two figured prominently in the plans and policies of Reza Shah, with priority given to the United States. The willingness of the Iranian government to grant oil concessions to American companies, and the engagement of Dr. Arthur C. Millspaugh as a financial consultant between 1922 and 1927 expressed Reza Shah's readiness to accept American influence. Basic American isolationism, however, impeded the development of greater participation by the United States. Accordingly, Reza Shah, fully conscious of the political implications of such an attitude, turned towards Germany.

Growth of German Influence

Iran began mining coal with modern methods only a few years before World War II. The machinery came from German firms; in fact, the Iranian Ministry of Mines and Industry purchased all factory installations for the production of coke and related coal products from Germany.

German companies constructed and supplied machinery for textile factories in Isfahan and Kerman, a paper factory in Isfahan, packing and drying establishments in various regions of Iran, and the only cement factory in the country.

In the field of electrical motors and light installations the famous Siemens Company enjoyed supremacy on the Iranian market. German technical assistance must be given credit for the development of the Iranian armaments industry, which included a machine gun factory in Tehran. German-Iranian cooperation in the munitions industry was only beginning when it was interrupted in 1941.

Solid foundations for trade had been established during the Weimar period and continued throughout the Nazi era. In 1929, Germany and Iran concluded a treaty of friendship and, by means of several conventions, regulated trade, tariffs, and navigation.

In the last year of the Weimar Republic (1932-33) Germany's share in Iran's foreign trade amounted to only 8 percent. During the Nazi period, as a result of skillful commercial policy, Germany attained an amazing growth. Dr.

Hjalmar Schacht, president of the Reichsbank and an economic expert, visited Iran in 1936 and concluded a trade agreement by which Germany was to supply Iran with railway material, machinery, and tools, taking in return raw wool and cotton.[5]

Germany's percentage of Iranian foreign trade increased rapidly—from 27 percent in 1936-37 to more than 40 percent in 1939-40. During this time, Soviet-Iranian trade fell into a slump. The Soviet Union accounted for 35.5 percent of all Iranian foreign trade from 1936 to 1937; by 1939-40 the Soviet share had diminished to 0.5 percent, a result of the lapsing of the commercial treaty in June 1938 which was apparently a consequence of the arrest of fifty-three Iranian Communists.[6]

The industrial development of Iran, largely under German influence after 1936, naturally brought a large number of German technicians into the country both to install machinery and to instruct Iranians in its use. They were to be found in all important factories, especially in electric power stations, steel factories, the textile trade, and in the post and telegraph stations. Some were in high positions in the railway administration, others were engineers in radio broadcasting stations, and still others were employed in the arsenal at Sultanatabad near Tehran.[7]

On the diplomatic front, the secret negotiations between the Germans and the Soviets during the period of Nazi-Soviet collaboration from 1939 to 1941, in which both parties sought to define their respective spheres of influence, registered the revival of Soviet aspirations *vis-à-vis* Iran.

During the Molotov-Hitler negotiations of November 1940, Germany proposed a settlement to Russia which would have included a delineation of German, Japanese, Italian, and Soviet spheres of interest and would have resulted in a pact partitioning the colonial heritage of the British Empire. Joachim von Ribbentrop suggested that "the focal points in the territorial aspirations of the Soviet Union would presumably be centered south of the territory of the Soviet Union in the direction of the Indian Ocean."[8] German intrigue in Iran notwithstanding, the Soviet foreign minister accepted this proposal with certain reservations, the most important of which read: "Provided that the area south of Batum and Baku in the general direction of the Persian Gulf is recognized as the center of the aspirations of the Soviet Union."[9] Although the German invasion of the USSR on 22 June 1941, precluded the implementation of such a program, it was not because the Soviet government and Nazi Germany disagreed on what to do with Iran or because the Soviet Union did not expect to obtain similar concessions from the Western Allies.

In the summer of 1941, the British watched the steady flow of Germans into Iran with alarm. Some of the Germans were specialists working for Iran's new Trans-Iranian Railway, in factories, and in public works. Others were archaeologists filled with wide-eyed interest in ancient Iran, and still others were tourists. According to British calculations Iran had a tight little nucleus of 3,000 Nazis,[10] although according to Iranian official sources there were only 664 German males employed in the country as of August 1941.[11]

Consequently, after the German invasion of the Soviet Union, the British and Soviet governments, now in alliance, started to pay greater heed to this potential German fifth column.

Anglo-Russian Invasion

The Iranian government formally declared its neutrality on 4 September 1939, following the outbreak of hostilities in Europe, and again on 26 June 1941, after the German attack on the Soviet Union. As the war spread to the Middle East, the Nazi-inspired *coup d'état* of Rashid Ali el-Gailani in neighboring Iraq in April 1941 gave a clear indication of Axis designs and influence in the Persian Gulf area. The Allies were determined to occupy Iran—without regard to that country's declared determination to remain neutral. The necessity of putting an end to Nazi fifth column activities was not, of course, the only concern of Allied strategy: India had to be protected against invasion from the north; also, Britain and Russia felt the need to provide a protected supply route for the support of the Soviet armed forces within Russia. Iran alone was capable of providing the necessary supply corridor.[12]

Equally vital to the Royal Navy were Iran's oil wells and the refineries close to the Persian Gulf, for much of the petroleum produced had been earmarked for Britain's ships and planes. It was with this in mind that Britain made overtures to Russia for a new agreement that would establish Russian and British zones of influence in Iran, shifting British forces from India to Iran to oppose any possible German drive through that country.[13]

Winston Churchill, the British prime minister, discussing this era wrote:

The need to pass munitions and supplies of all kinds to the Soviet Government and the extreme difficulties of the Arctic route, together with future strategic possibilities, made it eminently desirable to open the fullest communication with Russia through Persia. The Persian oil fields were a prime war factor. An active and numerous German mission had installed itself in Tehran and German prestige stood high. The suppression of the revolt in Iraq and the Anglo-French occupation of Syria, achieved as they were by narrow margins, blotted out Hitler's Oriental plan. We welcomed the opportunity of joining hands with the Russians and proposed to them a joint campaign. I was not without some anxiety about embarking on a Persian war, but the arguments for it were compulsive. I was very glad that General Wavell should be in India to direct the military movements.[14]

On 19 July 1941, one week after the signing of the Anglo-Soviet Agreement for Mutual Assistance, the two governments "drew the attention of the Persian Government to the large number of Germans in Persian territory and to the risk that they might compromise the neutrality of Persia by action against British and Russian interests—it was hoped that the Persian Government would arrange for the departure of Germans who gave no satisfactory reasons for their presence in the country."[15]

The Iranian government was understood to have replied on 29 July that the expulsion of German technicians would seriously affect Iran's normal relations with Germany, thus infringing upon Iran's neutrality as well as inviting German retaliation.[16]

The Russian government again warned that Iran's refusal to comply with Anglo-Russian demands for the expulsion of German agents and the purging of strong German influence might force the Soviets to send Red army troops into Iran, under Article VI of the Irano-Soviet Treaty of 1921.[17]

A treaty of friendship had been concluded in Moscow between Iran and Communist Russia on 26 February 1921. In it the Soviet government had declared ". . .the whole body of treaties and conventions concluded with Persia by the Tsarist Government, which crushed the rights of the Persian people, to be null and void."

Article VI, the most significant, which in the ensuing decades has plagued Iran, states that:

> If a third party should attempt to carry out a policy of usurpation by means of armed intervention in Persia, or if such power should desire to use Persian territory as a base of operations against Russia, or if a foreign power should threaten the frontiers of Federal Russia or those of its allies, and if the Persian Government should not be able to put a stop to such menace after having been once called upon to do so by Russia, Russia shall have the right to advance her troops into the Persian interior for the purpose of carrying out the military operations necessary for its defense. Russia undertakes, however, to withdraw her troops from Persian territory as soon as the danger has been removed.[18]

On 17 August notes were presented to the Iranian government by the Russian ambassador, Smirnov, and the British
minister, Sir Reader Bullard, this time *demanding* the
eviction of German technicians and experts in the service of
the Iranian government.

The Iranian reply to the Anglo-Russian note was delivered
on August 22. According to the official version, it declared
that Iran's policy had been to send away all foreigners whose
work could be done by Iranians. This policy was being carried
out more carefully and speedily as a result of Allied representation. "As the entry of all foreigners was controlled and
their conduct while in the country supervised. . . .the Allied
governments should feel no anxiety since nothing had
occurred to impair their interests."[19] The reply was termed
unsatisfactory by both London and Moscow, and tension between Iran and the Allies reached a critical stage.[20]

An examination of documents shows that the joint Anglo-
Russian notes of 17 August were for the record, and that the
Shah's government was facing a *fait accompli*. Reza Shah believed that the negotiations between his government and the
Allied governments would succeed. The Shah was convinced,
and the yes-men around him verified, that the British would
never invade Iran and that the Russians had their hands full
resisting German advances. But Churchill's memoirs reveal
that as early as 22 July General Quinan, who was commander
in Iraq, "had been ordered to be ready to occupy the oil
refinery at Abadan and the oil field, together with those two
hundred and fifty miles farther north near Khanagin."[21]

Churchill further asserts:

The next stage was to co-ordinate our plans, diplomatic and
military, with those of the Russians. On August 13, Mr.
Eden received Mr. Maisky* at the Foreign Office, and
terms of our respective Notes to Tehran were agreed. This
diplomatic move was to be our final word. Mr. Maisky told

* Russian Ambassador to England

the Foreign Secretary that 'after the presentation of the memoranda the Soviet Government would be ready to take military action, but they would not take such action except in conjunction with us.' On receiving this news I minuted (August 19), 'I think the Russian view is reasonable, and we ought to move with them while there is time.' We were now committed to action.[22]

German gains in southern Russia, which were seriously threatening both Odessa and Kiev, did not help the Allied position in the Middle East, where volatile governments were more impressed by military achievements than by diplomatic pleas or threats.

At dawn on 25 August 1941 the British minister, accompanied by the Soviet ambassador, appeared at the private residence of the Iranian prime minister, Ali Mansur, and informed him that Anglo-Russian forces had invaded Iran to wipe out the danger of a *coup d'état* by German agents.

The British explained their move by stating that:

The reply of the Iranian Government to communications addressed to them shows that they were not prepared to give adequate satisfaction to the recommendations of His Majesty's Government and the Soviet Union. It is clear that further friendly representations to the Iranian Government along the same lines would serve no useful purpose and that His Majesty's Government must have recourse to other measures to safeguard their essential interests. These measures will in no way be directed against the Iranian people. . . . but will be directed against attempts of the Axis powers to establish their control on Iran.[23]

The Soviet note, after detailing the friendship which the Soviet government claimed to have shown toward Iran, continued:

Recently, and especially since the treacherous attack of Hitler's Germans on the U.S.S.R., the alien activity of groups of Fascist German conspirators towards the U.S.S.R. and Iran on Iranian territory has reached menacing proportions. . . .German agents under the direction of the German Embassy in Tehran are organizing in a number of frontier places in Iran armed groups intended for Baku and other most important Soviet border places, with a view to arranging arson and explosions on the territory of the U.S.S.R. German agents have ammunition dumps at their disposal at different places in Iran. . . . The Soviet Government has three times warned the Iranian Government of the danger to its interests, as well as the interests of the U.S.S.R. and Great Britain. The Iranian Government has unfortunately refused to take measures which would put an end to the disturbances. . . .planned by German agents on the territory of Iran, thus encouraging these German agents in this criminal work. The Soviet Government has, therefore, been forced to take the necessary steps to implement its rights in accordance with paragraph six of the 1921 Agreement, and to introduce its troops on to the territory of Iran in self-defense. . . .The military measures now undertaken by the Soviet Government are directed exclusively against the danger produced by alien activity in Iran. As soon as the dangers threatening the interests of Iran and the U.S.S.R. have been averted, the Soviet Government will, in accordance with the undertakings given in the Soviet-Iranian Agreement of 1921, immediately withdraw its troops from the boundaries of Iran.[24]

Russian troops advanced through Azerbaijan as far as Rasht, Zanjan, and Rizaiya; at the same time, British and Indian forces rapidly took possession of the Abadan refinery, the railhead of Bandar Shahpur and, by the evening of 27 August, were halfway to Ahwaz and nearly at Kermanshah.

Reza Shah wanted to offer resistance, and a few shots were fired, but his army's collapse was complete. Reza's officers promptly either took off their uniforms or, if they did not have the time, just ran. As it turned out the officers lost more than their uniforms or their dignity: they were also deprived of most of the costly armaments that had helped them intimidate the Iranian people for more than twenty years.

How was such a swift disintegration of the army and the disruption of governmental institutions possible? For the answer, one must first examine the nature of Reza Shah's authority and the composition of the army and of the political and social groupings which were the mainstays of the Shah's power. (see table I).

The Nature of Reza Shah's Authority

Reza Shah's regime differed from other post-World War I totalitarian regimes. His did not have a political ideology, as did the Communist government in the Soviet Union or the Fascists in Italy, nor had he created a united mass movement as had Kemal Ataturk in Turkey.

Reza Shah's rule was authoritarian-personal. Absolute and ruthless, he spread fear among the people through the use of the security forces. Any power that stood in his way was mercilessly attacked and, when necessary, demolished.

However, Reza Shah did not annul the constitution, substitute decree for laws, abolish the cabinet, or destroy the Majlis—these survived. In practice, however, he acted completely contrary to the spirit of the constitution and violated many of its provisions, notably the bill of rights. Elections took place, but the Shah controlled them. The members of the Majlis passed laws, but strictly in accordance with the Shah's orders. The Prime Minister and other members of the government took their appointments and instructions from Reza Shah and resigned at his bidding. He destroyed such freedom of the press as had previously existed, as well as freedom of speech and assembly.

Reza Shah's repressive rule forced many people into apathy and drove others to corruption. The Shah found dishonest men more congenial and more willing to be his tools. In time,

Table 1

POLITICAL AND SOCIAL GROUPINGS*

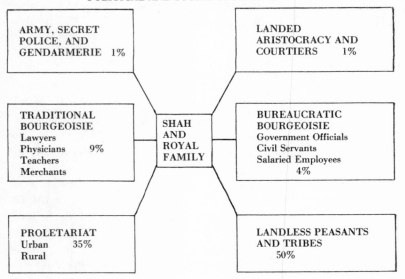

The estimates based on: Iranian Government, *Ministry of Interior*, Population Census, vol. I (Tehran: 1956).

*At the time of Reza Shah's abdication in September 1941.

he shunted aside his few upright advisors and surrounded himself with the worst elements of the country. These he made his accomplices, giving them privileges and favors. He rewarded vice and punished virtue with amazing thoroughness, at the same time presenting the Iranian people with a personal example of colossal corruption.[25]

The practice of terror also came naturally to Reza Shah. To quote from Arthur C. Millspaugh:

> Several prominent men, I was told, were poisoned in prison; for example Firouz (Nosrat al-Dowleh), former Minister of Finance; Teymour Tash, once the trusted Minister of the Court; Sardar Assad, a chief of the Bakhtiari who at one time had been Minister of War. Davar,.... an exceptionally able official (Minister of Justice and Finance), committed suicide....Fear settled upon the people. No one knew whom to trust; and none dared to protest or criticize.[26]

Others who were killed by the order of Reza Shah included Modares, a member of the Majlis and a religious leader; Sardar Fateh and Sardar Eqbal, Chiefs of the Bakhtiari tribe; Solat ud-Dolah, Chief of the Qashqai tribe; and Dr. Taghi Erani, physicist from Azerbaijan. Dr. Mohammed Mussadeq, former minister and Majlis deputy, was imprisoned.

The Security Forces

The rank and file of the soldiers were conscripts. Those recruited were illiterate peasants from the countryside and poor city dwellers. Reza Shah, from the outset, persuaded the Majlis to enact a law calling for two years of compulsory military service for all men upon reaching the age of twenty-one. This regulation was unevenly enforced, since the children of the rich and influential were able to stay out of the army by either attending educational institutions or buying an exemption through bribery.

The officer corps had no ideological commitment. Many of the senior officers were corrupt, ill-trained, and illiterate. Many were the Shah's old cronies who had no concept of how to lead or train an efficient modern army. Nevertheless, under an authoritarian and hierarchial decisional structure, their power was immense.[27]

Many had amassed great wealth by stealing from the provisions allotted to the recruits and from appropriations for the purchase of weapons.[28]

The socioeconomic background of the junior officers was lower middle class. A number had been trained in France and Germany, while others attended either of the two military academies in Tehran which were under the direction of French officers in the early 1930s. Promotion was based on personal influence and political reliability. It was a submissive military elite, its major role being either to spy on the civilian population in the cities or to act as military governors in the tribal areas.

Under Reza Shah's policy of giving priority to the armed forces, approximately one-third of the total national revenue each year was allocated for that purpose. When this most expensive organization was called upon to defend the nation, it crumbled on the first day of the British-Soviet invasion.[29]

The gendarmerie, an army-controlled security force, was responsible for the security of the roads and the countryside. Its commander was a senior army officer, and its total force was estimated at twelve thousand. As an emergency measure, after the outbreak of World War II, the gendarmerie had been absorbed into the regular army.[30]

As for its effectiveness, the force lacked discipline and training and was the most corrupt group in the country. The rank and file received low pay and lived off what they could extort from the villagers or travelers.

The police force was national and centralized. It had been organized in 1910 by a group of Swedish officers. In 1923, Reza Shah dismissed the Swedish officers and appointed a senior army officer, Colonel Mohammed Khan Dargahy, with no experience in police operations, to head the force. Most of the senior police officers were also appointed from the army. Reza Shah's actions made the police a valuable arm of his military dictatorship.[31] Police power was unlimited. The fear it created in the cities was unprecedented, for no citizen was immune from blackmail, torture, or assassination.

After Reza Shah's fall, Mukhtari, the Chief of Police (along with ten of his associates), and Ahmadi, Tehran's prison doctor, were tried for torture, poisonings, and scores of political murders. Ahmadi was hanged, and the rest received sentences of from ten years to life imprisonment.[32]

Landed Aristocracy

The rise of Reza Shah brought a change in the makeup of the landowning class. The old landed proprietors and tribal khans began to lose their land and villages. Reza Shah's policy of land confiscation especially weakened the position and power of the tribal khans, and reduced their economic status to such an extent that they were often forced to sell other property. For example, the Bakhtiari properties in certain parts of Khuzistan were sold in part when the tribal fortunes declined under Reza Shah.

The various changes in land ownership helped develop a new landed class composed of bureaucrats, military personnel, and merchants. This was a *nouveau riche* group who had either received their land from the Shah or who, in their position as government officials, civil and military, had acquired property in the areas where they had held office. This applied to all ranks from sergeant or private in the gendarmerie to governor-general.[33]

Iranian merchants invested in land either for its economic value or, even more, for the political power and social prestige which the ownership of property conferred. As in any primitive economy, land was looked upon as a source of gain, whether in the form of social prestige, political power, or economic advantage. Among all types of landowners, the tendency to prefer extent to quality was widespread. Thus it would probably not be unfair to say that the average Iranian landowner would rather have owned several villages in bad condition than one or a few in good condition.[34]

There was a wide gulf between the landowners as a class, no matter what their origin, and the peasants. In no sense was there a spirit of cooperation or a feeling of being engaged in a mutual enterprise. The attitude on the whole was one of shared suspicion. The landlord virtually regarded the peasant as a drudge whose function was to provide him with his profits and who would, if treated with anything but rigidity, cheat him out of his gains. Education, better hygiene, and improved housing for the peasant were regarded as unnecessary, except by a minority of the more enlightened landowners.[35]

The landlords, fearing land reform and desiring to establish an alliance with Reza Shah, presented him with several of their villages. The Shah developed a healthy appetite for land-ownership, and before long he was to become the proprietor of large estates covering the provinces of Mazanderan, Gorgan, and Gilan.

Of course, this alliance was of great benefit to the landlords since they utilized the assistance of the army and gendarmerie to prevent any change in the feudal system and to quell any uprisings on the part of peasants. Accordingly, the Reza Shah tolerated the landowners just so long as he received absolute obedience from them and had his dictatorial desires carried out.[36]

Reza Shah, at the time of his abdication, had become the largest landholder in the country, and twenty years of his regime had perpetuated a system of semiserfdom for the peasants. Nor were there any positive channels in the decision-making procedure for the landlords.[37]

Bureaucratic Bourgeoisie

On 12 December 1922, the Fourth Majlis had enacted the first legislation regulating civil service in Iran. Based on Western models, the law established age, education, and character qualifications for prospective civil servants. It also outlined a table of ranks and called for competitive entrance examinations. It established penalties for corrupt practice and allowed for the dismissal of incompetents.[38]

American advisors were hired to help with the organization of the civil service. Soon after Reza Khan attained power he fired the Americans and, under his autocratic rule, established control over the appointment of all ministers, governors, mayors, police officials, and other municipal officials. He initiated a deliberate campaign of glorification of the state, which imputed a high degree of social prestige to men in government service although the earnings of civil servants from the lowest to the highest rank were always at minimal levels. Graft and bribery became a permanent fixture of government operations. All ranks, ministers as well as minor clerks, were involved. The law had little effect on the custom of *rushveh* "bribe". From traffic police to governors and ministers, it varied only in magnitude. Those who did not participate were often ostracized.[39]

The Shah had set the example, and every officer, governor, or cabinet member practiced autocracy, favoritism, and corruption in the areas of his responsibility.[40]

Traditional Bourgeoisie

In a society historically feudal and illiterate to a great extent, the educated came to be accepted as an inevitable minority. Literacy was very uncommon and consequently prized, and schooling, regardless of content or level of proficiency, therefore became the means by which individuals achieved membership in the group of the educated elite. A man remained a member of that group by virtue of having been educated, whether or not he worked and no matter what he contributed to society.[41]

Reza Shah's regime proposed to increase the rate of literacy and to modernize the Iranian society. Beginning in 1928, using funds appropriated by the Majlis, 100 students were sent annually to Europe (predominantly France). A smaller number were sent to Germany, and by 1934-35 the returning graduates had become the foundation for the structure of governmental administration. They were also responsible for the establishment of Tehran University. At the same time, secondary schools and colleges were created to train teachers, lawyers, and physicians.[42]

The teaching staff of Tehran University, with the exception of some old scholars of Persian literature and Arabic, had been generally trained in France. There was also a considerable number of European professors.

Standards at the schools of medicine, engineering, and law were generally adequate to meet the needs of the nation, but in the social sciences the standards were very low. The professor would read a lecture—often translated from a French text—and the students would take verbatim notes. In the preparation for examination, a memorization of these notes was all that was necessary. Traditions and standards of scholarship, academic integrity, and intellectual discipline were seldom practiced. No attempt was made to train for responsibility, independence, or truth-searching.[43]

Consequently, the system incubated an "educated" man who was primarily, although not exclusively, a political animal. He was a good memorizer who spoke well, but not concretely; who was quick to copy and serve those in authority; who hated to make decisions; who was not objective; who could not operate effectively in a critical environment; who could not analyze his responsibilities; and who was basically insecure and maladjusted to any of his occupational demands and was thus, unproductive: in short, an individual who was the very antithesis of the educated or sophisticated individual required to participate in the building of a modern society.[44]

Proletariat—Landless Peasants

Reza Shah's regime had no effect on improving the wretched conditions of the peasants or the proletariat. On the contrary, since the Shah feared the development of political, social, and economic consciousness among the workers and the peasants exploitative legislation was enacted for the control of the two groups.

The peasants of Iran were engaged in subsistence agriculture in traditionally oriented rural villages, which were seldom completely self-sufficient. Their relations with the landowner were based mostly on crop-sharing agreements.[45]

The crop-sharing method was founded on local custom and differed in detail considerably from district to district. Traditionally, five elements were taken into account in dividing the crop: land, water, seed, animals, and labor. In theory, one share was allotted to each element and went to whoever provided that element. However, this was little more than a theoretical abstraction, and the division was seldom made on the basis of the allotment of five equal shares for each element. In many areas the position of the peasant could best be described as one of continual servitude.[46]

For the peasants who worked on the estates of the Shah, there were added problems. For example, no one could move off the property without written permission from the kadkhuda ("village supervisor").

The plight of the peasantry can be further illustrated by figures compiled from one of the most fertile areas, Demavand-Tehran. During this period, sixty percent of the peasants owned no land; twenty five percent had less than two acres; and fifteen percent possessed about two acres.[47]

In 1930 the Shah intensified his efforts to industrialize the nation. Private initiative in this field was encouraged, and laws were passed giving preferential treatment to individuals who would establish private factories. Although some advantage was taken of these statutes (the creation of the textile industry in Isfahan, for example), certain factors militated against private entrepreneurial activity in Iran: the lack of sufficient capital, the contentment of the landowning class, a tendency to invest savings in real estate, a lack of faith in any long-range political stability, and serious doubts about the willingness or the ability of the government to protect private investments.[48]

It became obvious from the start that industrialization could be undertaken only by direct state action. It is not intended here to present complete data on the industrialization of Iran, but Reza Shah himself became active in this sector by establishing textile factories and sugar refineries on his estates. A rural labor force was recruited from the farms of these areas. Working for the Shah, they were placed under absolute control in regard to their movement or pay.

In general, restrictive labor laws stifled any move on the part of the workers either to pursue union activity or to organize strikes, and it became the general lot of the urban and rural workers to live in dirty, poor housing and in massive impoverishment.[49]

Preference for nonmanual desk jobs over manual employment attested to the traditional Iranian attitude toward work. Most typically, labor was considered as suitable only for servants and casual employees of the educated wealthy. Quite understandably, this attitude toward manual labor had a detrimental effect on the development of a pool of motivated and skilled workers so necessary for Reza Shah to succeed with his program for economic development.[50]

Under such conditions, when the test came for the army and the civilian leaders to organize and fight and make sacrifices for the country, they showed no initiative or purpose.

The structure which was built on terror and corruption crumbled. The Allied invasion and the pathetic dissolution of the much-heralded Iranian armed forces produced intense shock, disorganization, and disorder throughout the nation. On 27 August 1941, Ali Mansur resigned and was replaced by Mohammed Ali Foroughi as prime minister.[51]

On 30 August an Allied note was delivered which required the Iranian government to expel all German citizens within one week. It accepted the continuance of the Axis diplomatic establishment and the continued residence of a limited number of essential German technicians. In reply, the Iranian government asked for a revision of the boundaries of the proposed British and Soviet zones of occupation and an indemnity for the loss of Iranian life and property. A week later stiffer terms were demanded by the Allied governments, embodied in an agreement, published in London on 9 September, to which the Iranian Majlis meekly submitted on the same day. This accord provided for the closing of the German, Italian, Hungarian, and Rumanian legations and the surrender of all Axis nationals. It mentioned the continuance of British and Russian payments for the oil and Caspian fisheries concessions, and established the nominal limits of British and Russian occupation. The British zone was to include the whole of the Anglo-Iranian oil-fields from the Persian Gulf north of Khanaqin and Kermanshah. The Soviet zone included the Iranian northwest, with Tabriz as its center, and extended eastward around the southern shore of the Caspian to the railhead at Bandar Shah and southward to Qazvin and Semnan but not to Tehran.[52]

While the British note expressed readiness to discuss the boundary provisions and the payment of an indemnity for the loss of Iranian life and property, at the final evacuation the Soviet government refused to make alterations in its zone boundary, to pay an indemnity, or to return captured arms and ammunition.

The lesson of big power politics, painfully learned by the

Iranians in the decade beginning in 1907 and happily forgotten
after 1917, had again been brought forcefully to their attention.
The settlement imposed upon the Shah went far beyond the
earlier demands that German agents be expelled, and it opened
wide the possibilities both for the defense of the Soviet Union
and for the security of the British position in the Middle East.
H. W. Baldwin, commenting on the invasion, wrote:

> Earlier this year there appeared strong likelihood that the
> Germans would pour into Africa and Asia Minor. But the
> German drive on Suez halted at the Egyptian frontier; the
> pro-Nazi putsch in Iraq ended in the British invasion and
> occupation of the country and Syria also was occupied. Iran
> was the gap in a territorial situation that extended from Egypt
> to India. With the Anglo-Russian occupation of Iran, the
> British 'front' now extends unbroken from Libya to
> Baluchistan and the Western frontiers of India.[53]

Winston Churchill summed up the situation as follows:

> Thus ended this brief and fruitful exercise of overwhelming
> force against a weak and ancient state. Britain and Russia
> were fighting for their lives. *Inter arma silent leges*. We may
> be glad that in our victory the independence of Persia has
> been preserved. Persian resistance had collapsed so swiftly
> that our contacts with the Kremlin became again almost
> entirely political. Our main object in proposing the joint
> Anglo-Russian campaign in Persia had been to open up the
> communications from the Persian Gulf to the Caspian
> Sea. . . . We were of course both agreed on the expulsion from
> Persia or capture of all Germans and the wiping-out of
> German influence and intrigues in Tehran and elsewhere.
> The deep and delicate question of oil, Communism, and the
> post-war future of Persia lay in the background, but need not
> it seemed to me, impede comradeship and good-will.[54]

Iran Under Occupation

At the beginning of the occupation Britain wanted to keep
Tehran neutral, provided the Shah embraced all its demands.

In a telegram to Sir Reader Bullard, the British minister, Winston Churchill stated, "We hope it will not be necessary, in the present phase at any rate, to have an Anglo-Russian occupation of Teheran, but the Persian Government will have to give us loyal and faithful help and show all proper alacrity if they wish to avoid it. At the present time we have not turned against the Shah, but unless good results are forthcoming his misgovernment of his people will be brought into account." Churchill also demanded: ". . .Our requirements must somehow be met, and it ought to be possible for you to obtain all the facilities we require, bit by bit, by using the leverage of a possible Russian occupation of Teheran. There is no need to fear undue Russian encroachments, as their one supreme wish will be to get the through route for American supplies."[55]

It was in this connection that Churchill told Stalin on 16 September 1941:

> I am anxious to settle our alliance with Persia and to make an intimate efficient working arrangement with your forces in Persia. There are in Persia signs of serious disorder among tribesmen and of breakdown of Persian authority. Disorder, if it spreads, will mean wasting our divisions holding down these people. . .Our object should be to make the Persians keep each other quiet while we get on with the war. Your Excellency's decisive indications in this direction will speed forward the already favourable trend of our affairs in this minor theatre.[56]

The Iranian attitude, dictated by the angry and sullen Reza Shah, was still defiant, and an editorial of 10 September in the official newspaper *Ettelaat* deplored the closing of Axis legations. It chided the Allies for impossible demands and asked the Iranian government to continue its political relations with Germany, Japan, and Italy, and to keep open its missions in those countries. This editorial provoked Allied protest.

On 15 September the Russians advanced on Tehran from the north as the British advanced from the south. The next day Reza Shah abdicated and left for Isfahan. The ground for his departure had been prepared by BBC messages broadcast in Persian from London between 13 and 15 September. With even greater outspokenness, they reminded listeners of the increasingly autocratic nature of the Shah's regime and placed responsibility for Persia's recent troubles on the Shah and his Nazi-like government. These broadcasts were reported to have met with a favourable reception in Tehran.

The twenty-two year old Crown Prince, Mohammed Reza, was now proclaimed Shah. On 20 September he restored the constitutional monarchy and, in the following days, declared that the properties inherited from his father would be devoted to the welfare of the nation. He issued a decree of amnesty to all political prisoners.[57]

The ex-Shah wished to go to India. He was unpopular with the Indian Muslims due to his harsh regimentation of Islam in Persia, and the Indian government therefore thought it unwise to have him there. He was first taken by the British to Mauritius Island and later to South Africa, where he died in Johannesburg on 26 July 1944.[58]

Negotiations for a Tripartite Treaty of Alliance among the Soviet Union, England, and Iran began in September 1941, and were concluded on 29 January 1942. According to this Treaty the two powers agreed to guarantee the territorial integrity, the sovereignty, and political independence of Iran and to withdraw their forces from the territory of Iran "not later than six months" after the termination of all hostilities. It was agreed that the Iranian armed forces would not be required to take part in military operations against any foreign power, only to maintain internal security on Iranian territory. The Allied Powers were given the unrestricted right to use and, in case of military necessity, to control all means of communication throughout Iran for the passage of troops or supplies from one Allied power to the other. Iran conceded to the Allies the right to maintain on its soil land, sea, and air forces in such manner as they considered necessary, but it was understood that the presence of these forces did not constitute a military occupation. The Allied Powers also agreed to safeguard the Iranian economy against wartime difficulties and to open negotiations with the Iranian government to this effect.[59] World War II brought much hardship to Iran. From the outset the Soviet Union sealed off northern Iran from the rest of the country, blocking the free flow of goods between the north and the south. Bread, meat, and other staples were in short supply, largely because of the requirements of the Russian, British, and American service units which operated the supply route from the Persian Gulf to the Soviet Union. The dislocation of the transportation system was a major factor in the aggravation of near-famine conditions in certain areas where there were local food shortages. In addition, much of the grain surplus of Azerbaijan was sent to Russia, and Anglo-American relief measures became necessary to avert widespread starvation. The Soviet Union was in grave danger, and the exclusive concern of Soviet policy in the Middle East was therefore to utilize the resources and transit facilities of the area to defeat Germany.[60]

Soviet forces in Iran were estimated to be between 85 thousand and 100 thousand. Equipment included 150 tanks and 200 pieces of heavy artillery. The Soviets established two headquarters: the first in Tabriz, the capital of the Azerbaijan province; the other in Qazvin, a city 80 miles to the north of Tehran.[61] The occupied area covered approximately 250 thousand square miles composed of the province of Azerbaijan, Gilan, Mazanderan, Khorasan, Zanjan, Gorgan, and Qazvin. Some troops were also stationed outside Tehran.[62]

The ruling landlords and their upper bourgeois associates living in the north were in a state of fear and shock. Because of the many years of Reza Shah's anti-Communist propaganda and his efficient suppression of the Communist party, the privileged classes associated Soviet occupation with death, rape, and plunder. Panic-stricken, many high governmental officials, army generals, and prosperous landowners left hurriedly for Tehran and the southern provinces.[63]

To the surprise of many, the Red Army was the most disciplined of the three occupying forces. The officers had absolute control over their troops, and on several occasions soldiers were executed for the crimes of rape or stealing from the local population.[64]

Soviet actions made a good impression on the Iranians, and there was much praise within the Majlis and in the newspapers for the generally good behavior of the Soviet officers and troops. Meanwhile, the same sources criticized the actions of British and Indian soldiers in the southern provinces.[65]

On 28 February 1944, an editorial in the newspaper *Mehan** ("Fatherland") indicated that "compared to the British and American forces, the behavior of Soviet troops has been so magnificent that there is now a threat to the sovereignty of the nation. . . .One fears, that on the day the Russians are ready to leave Iran, there will be a serious demand from the Iranian people that they should remain indefinitely."

In the early stages of the occupation the Soviet authorities were very careful not to interfere directly with day-to-day work in the provinces. They helped local officials and police forces to establish order and invited the army, gendarmerie, and police officers who had fled to return.

The Soviets moved with caution in changing the agricultural structure. The estates of the big landowners, which had been left with caretakers, were not confiscated, and there was no immediate evidence of land reform. One early move was to issue a new regulation which favored the peasantry, as opposed to the landlords, with regard to the sharing of crops.[66]

In the field of administration, the Russians made it clear that designated Iranian representatives must acquiesce fully to their demands and receive the approval of the Soviets for

* The editor of *Mehan* was anti-Communist.

any offical actions. Accordingly, when Dr. A. C. Millspaugh, the financial administrator to the government of Iran, wanted to dispatch his American assistants to the provinces of Khorasan and Azerbaijan to collect back taxes, the Soviet authorities refused to issue the necessary permits. It became obvious to all that, without their permission, no one could travel beyond Qazvin.[67]

The Soviet consul in each province became the intermediary between the Iranians and the Red Army officers. The consuls spoke fluent *Farsi*, and most had spent many years in Iran. All consuls received their instructions from the Soviet ambassador in Tehran, who also handled the many communications from the Iranian Government. In the event of major disputes between the two countries, a special emissary was dispatched from Moscow.[68]

Soviet propaganda was extensively and effectively organized. The Russian ambassador, Smirnov, contacted members of parliament, editors of newspapers, and many anti-Reza Shah intellectuals, who had recently been released from prison, to explain that the Soviet presence in Iran was not an occupation but a culmination of Article VI of the 1921 treaty. Its goal was to preserve effectively the sovereignty of Iran, with the eradication of German elements and of their ally, the tyrant Reza Shah. He emphasized that it was with Soviet support that Reza Shah had been deposed and constitutional government restored. The ambassador also explained that the Russians supported the aspirations and desires of the progressive Iranians and would help the nation achieve its economic independence from the British, who at that time held the concession for the southern oil fields.[69]

Another important vehicle of Soviet propaganda was the Irano-Soviet Society for Cultural Relations, founded in the fall of 1943. The Society, headed by Ali Asghar Hekmat, a former minister of education, included among its associates many Iranian scholars and scientists. Bahar, the poet laureate of Iran, and Dehkhuda, a prominent figure in the field of literature and the author of the *Iranian Encyclopedia*, were two notable members. The Society held lavish parties and receptions and actively distributed Soviet literature, newspapers, and films.

The Russians also established a hospital in Tehran equipped with excellent medical facilities and directed by competent doctors. It was open to the public and was free for the poor. Much needed drugs and vaccines were distributed to Iranian patients through the Society for Cultural Relations.[70]

During this period more than 500 politicians, journalists, landowners, clergymen, lawyers, army officers, and merchants were arrested and detained by the British and the Soviets in their respective zones. Most were charged with pro-German activities and were interned throughout the war. Some of the arrested, such as General Zahedi (who later became prime minister after a *coup d'état* against Dr. Mussadeq in 1953), were imprisoned by the British in Palestine.[71]

On 9 September 1943, after the German retreat from Russia was well under way, Iran declared war on Germany. At the end of November, Roosevelt, Churchill, and Stalin arrived in Iran to attend the Tehran Conference. The resulting Tehran Declaration again reaffirmed the sovereignty and territorial integrity of the nation and stated that after the cessation of hostilities the three powers would give full consideration to the grim economic problems facing Iran.[72]

Notes

1. M. Bahar, *Tarikh-e Mokhtasar-e Ahzab-e Siyasiye Iran* [A short history of the political parties of Iran] (Tehran: Sherkat-e Sahami Chap, 1944), pp. 72-75 (hereafter cited as *Short History*).

2. Ibid., pp. 85-87, 101-2; Hussein Makki, *Tarikh-e Bist Salleh Iran* [Twenty years history of Iran], 3 vols., (Tehran: Majlis Press, 1946-47), 2:281, 2:287, 2:297-305. (Hereafter cited as *Twenty Years History*).

3. Makki, *Twenty Years History* 3:367-88, 3:468-75.

4. Ibid., 3:580-86; *Mozakerat Majlis* [Majlis debates] (Tehran), 12 December 1925.

5. George Lenczowski, *Russia and The West in Iran* (Ithaca, N.Y.: Cornell University Press, 1949), pp. 152-61.

6. Ivar Spector, *The Soviet Union and the Muslim World* (Seattle: University of Washington Press, 1959), p. 187.

7. *New York Times*, 18 August 1941.

8. R. J. Sontag and J. S. Beddie, eds., *Nazi-Soviet Relations, 1939-1941: Documents from the Archives of the German Foreign Office*, (New York: Didier, 1948), p. 250.

9. Ibid., pp. 258-59.

10. *Time*, 1 September 1941, p. 18.

11. *Ettelaat*, 22 August 1941.

12. Christina Phelps Grant, "Iran: Test of Relations Between Great and Small Nations," *Foreign Policy Reports*, vol. 21, no. 3 (15 April 1945), p. 32.

13. *New York Times*, 2 July 1941.

14. Winston S. Churchill, *The Grand Alliance, The Second World War* (Boston: Houghton Mifflin Company, 1950), p. 477.

15. George Kirk, *The Middle East in the War, Survey of International Affairs, 1939-1946*, 3 vols. (London: Oxford University Press, 1952), 2:133.

16. Ibid.

17. *New York Times*, 12 August 1941.

18. J. C. Hurewitz, *Diplomacy in the Near and Middle East* (Princeton: D. Van Nostrand Company, Inc.: 1956), pp. 90-91. For the text in *Farsi* see Manshur Garagani, *Siasate Dowlate Showravi Dar Iran as 1296-1306* [The policy of the Soviet government in Iran from 1917-1929] (Tehran: Chapkhaneh Mozaheri), pp. 123-30.

19. Kirk, *The Middle East*, 2:134.

20. *New York Times*, 24 August 1941.

21. Churchill, *The Grand Alliance*, p. 481.

22. Ibid., p. 480.

23. *New York Times*, 26 August 1941.

24. Test taken from British Broadcasting Corporation: *Daily Digest of Foreign Broadcasts*, no. 769 (August 26, 1941), cited in Kirk, *The Middle East*, 2:135-136.

25. Arthur C. Millspaugh, *Americans in Persia* (Washington: The Brookings Institution, 1946), pp. 36-37.

26. Ibid.

27. Ebrahim Khajeh Nouri, *Bazigaran-e Asr-e Talaie, Soheili* [The actors of the golden age, Soheili] (Tehran: Adalat Newspaper Publication, 1320/1941), pp. 464-67.

28. Ibid.

29. Abdlsamad Kambakhsh, *Nazari Be Jumbesh Kargari Va Communist Dar Iran* [A glance at the Communist labor movement in Iran] (Publication of Tudeh Party of Iran, 1972), pp. 49-50. (hereafter cited as *Communist Labor Movement*).

30. J. C. Hurewitz, *Middle East Politics: The Military Dimension* (New York: Praeger Publishers, 1970), p. 272.

31. Bahar, *Short History*, pp. 283-86.

32. Kambakhsh, *Communist Labor Movement*, pp. 37, 51.

33. Ann K. S. Lambton, *Landlord and Peasants in Persia* (London: Oxford University Press, 1953), pp. 259-62.

34. Ibid.

35. Ibid., p. 263.

36. Kambakhsh, *Communist Labor Movement*, pp. 38-39.

37. Ibid.

38. Amin Banani, *The Modernization of Iran, 1921-1941* (Stanford: Stanford University Press, 1961), p. 59.

39. Ibid., pp. 60-61.

40. Makki, *Twenty Years History*, 2:79-80.

41. Norman Jacobs, *The Sociology of Development, Iran as an Asian Case Study* (New York: Frederick A. Praeger, 1966), p. 153.

42. Banani, *Modernization*, p. 94-95.

43. Ibid., pp. 99-100.

44. Jacobs, *Sociology of Development*, pp. 158-59.

45. Lambton, *Landlords and Peasants*, p. 306.

46. Ibid.

47. Kambakhsh, *Communist Labor Movement*, pp. 47-48.

48. Banani, *Modernization*, p. 138.

49. Kambakhsh, *Communist Labor Movement*, p. 49.

50. Jacobs, *Sociology of Development*, p. 169.

51. *Newsweek*, 8 September 1941.

52. Thomas Brockway, "The Purge of Iran," *Current History* (October 1941), pp. 160-63.

53. H. W. Baldwin, "Middle East Strategy," *New York Times*, 26 August 1941, p. 4.

54. Churchill, *The Grand Alliance*, pp. 482-83.

55. Ibid., p. 484.

56. Ibid.

57. Kirk, *The Middle East*, 2:138.

58. Ibid.

59. For the full text of the Treaty see Hurewitz, *Diplomacy*, pp. 232-34.

60. Richard W. Cottam, *Nationalism in Iran* (Pittsburgh: University of Pittsburgh Press, 1967), p. 196.

61. *Eqdam*, 27 October 1944.

62. Ibid.

63. *Iran Ma*, 15 September 1943.

64. *Khandaniha*, 8 September 1944.

65. *Eqdam*, 18 September 1944.

66. *Khandaniha*, 21 February 1944.

67. Ibid.

68. *Qeyam Iran*, 21 February 1944.

69. *Bakhtar*, 25 October 1943.

70. Spector, *USSR and the Muslim World*, p. 196.

71. *Keyhan*, 12 February 1943.

72. "Statement on Iran, American War Documents," *Current History*, (January 1944), p. 54.

2 The Oil Controversy

The Shah's abdication and the resulting loosening of restrictions following the Anglo-Soviet invasion in August 1941 brought enormous relief to the country. The controlling Allied forces were preoccupied with the emergencies of war and as a result, for a brief period at least, the Iranians enjoyed unaccustomed political latitude.

Both British and Soviet authorities declared that the presence of their troops did not constitute an occupation and, therefore, the Iranian government could continue to function. However, at the head of the government was a young, inexperienced Shah, whose authority was largely ignored.

At that time the Majlis consisted of 136 members. The vast majority of deputies in the Majlis represented powerful cliques—the court, the clergy, the army, and the propertied classes—whose interests they were expected to advance along with their own. As the deputies moved in and out of the numerous factions (then commonly known as *Fraction*), the Majlis was in a state of continuous flux. The cabinet ministers, who had to rely upon the support of a majority in the Majlis for their political life, were, as a rule, older men who took turns in office and whose participation in government was merely an effective way of enhancing personal and family interests. Profiting from their positions, they were opposed to change.[1]

Public dissatisfaction with the deputies broke out immediately after Reza Shah's abdication. They were accused of buying their seats, of giving and taking bribes, of using their positions for personal and family profit. Some were often absent, and others were said to be too ignorant and uninformed to understand the laws on which they voted or the problems of the country as a whole.

Much of the attack on the ministers and deputies came from the newspapers. Once Reza Shah was gone, hundreds of newspapers and news sheets containing lofty sermons about democracy and social revolution flooded Tehran. Some had a miniscule circulation and quickly folded after two or three issues. Other papers were supported by the Soviet and British authorities.[2]

The disruptive atmosphere within Iranian society prompted the Soviets to reassess their policies toward Iran. In Marxist-Leninist thinking, Iran was considered a weak, semicolonial nation in the feudal stage of historical development subject to exploitation by western capitalistic societies at the imperialistic stage. Socialist Russia, at least during the war, had to cooperate in Iran with capitalist America and Britain because Soviet survival depended upon military, economic, and technical assistance from the United States. But the Soviet Union had three ultimate objectives in Iran: (1) containment of British and American influence; (2) maintenance of friendly relations with the government; and (3) the establishment of an indigenous revolutionary Communist organization.

In this connection it is essential to examine four factors: (1) the formation of the Communist *Tudeh* Party "the Masses"; (2) the role of the Fourteenth Majlis; (3) Kavtaradze and the oil question; and (4) Dr. Mussadeq and the neutralization of the major powers.

The Tudeh Party

In the mid-1930s, Dr. Taghi Erani, a Berlin-educated physicist from Azerbaijan, had organized a group of Western-educated Iranians for the purpose of circulating Marxist ideas in Iran. During this period, when open Communist Party activity was forbidden, Erani had published the journal *Donya* "World", which became the circle's theoretical journal.

Donya followed an unswerving Marxist interpretation of history and political philosophy. Its views of the state and of class interest and conflict typified its orientation. "The state," wrote Erani in an essay on the materialistic view of man, was "an apparatus organized by the most powerful class to ensure its domination of the weaker classes." Since both the legislative and the judiciary systems, as well as education and the arts, were under the control of the state, Erani concluded that in a class society every aspect of social and political life was class based and organized in the interest of the dominant group. Thus, it was foolish to think that such an organization could ever bring happiness and prosperity to all. Erani stressed that such conditions finally resulted in class struggle and revolution.[3]

To further explain the concept of dialectic materialism, Erani wrote that in nature everything is in a state of change; tranquility and stagnation do not exist. Continuous transformation, evolution, and permanent modernization are natural laws. Applying this principle to society, Erani claimed that the history of human society is the history of the class struggle. He added: "Contrast and struggle are mothers of every progress."[4]

Erani's followers, who often met in groups to discuss his ideas, were recruited from among teachers, students, lawyers, judges, and the proletariat. More than sixty five percent belonged to the middle class, fifteen percent to the upper bourgeoise, and twenty percent to the lower bourgeoise. Professionally, the group contained thirty five percent teachers, twenty five percent lawyers and government employees (including judges), fifteen percent students, fifteen percent workers, and ten percent others.[5]

In April 1937, Dr. Erani and fifty-two of the most prominent members of the circle were arrested and charged with conspiring to violate the Anti-Communist Act of 1931. During their public trial, held from 2 November to 13 November of that year, articles from *Donya* were cited to prove the group's engagement in Communist propaganda in violation of the law. However, all of the defendants claimed that by studying the journal and reading other relevant literature they had merely learned about dialectic materialism and modern social theories. Dr. Erani spoke vigorously in his own defense, contending that the Law of 1931 violated every principle of justice and was clearly unconstitutional; that he had merely advocated dialectic materialism; and that the court was incompetent to try him, because it was the tool of the state and in conspiracy with the police.

The trial ended with the conviction of the fifty-three defendants. Ten of the leaders received the maximum penalty of ten years; the others received terms ranging from three to seven years in prison. Erani's death in the prison hospital on 4 February 1940, is believed to have been precipitated by the deliberate negligence of hospital authorities.[6]

The imprisonment of the Erani circle proved to be of considerable value to the movement as a whole, for in prison indoctrination continued relentlessly. The hard core became more than ever dedicated to Communism and many young members, in their student years when arrested, turned the prison cells into classes of Communist education.

The amnesty declared by Mohammed Reza Shah in September 1941 released from prison prominent members of the Erani circle, who organized the *Tudeh* Party ("the Masses") the following month. Among its founders were former prisoners, Dr. Reza Radmanesh, Dr. Fereidoun Keshavarz, Dr. Morteza Yazdi, Ali Bozorg Alavi, Dr. Mohammed Bahrami (its Marxist theoretician), and Reza Rusta, who became famous through his organization of the workers of the Anglo-Iranian Oil Company. It chose Soleiman Mohsen Eskandari, a respectable liberal prince of the Qajar dynasty, as the chairman of a "Provisional Committee of Fifteen," which included two of his nephews, Iraj and Abbas Eskandari.[7] Jafar Pishevari was later to join the party.

In its formative years, the Tudeh Party avoided mention of Communism and insisted that it had no ties with the Soviet Union. The provisional statute of the new organization described it as a mass organization based on a union of workers, peasants, intellectual democrats, and artisans, a democratic and progressive party seeking major structural reforms of economic, political, and social institutions and finally, an anti-imperialist organization fighting foreign intervention and colonialism.[8]

Conditions were ripe for the growth of the party—a mass of exploited workers and landless peasants, a small middle class of discontented and frustrated intellectuals, a few hundred rich families controlling all the wealth, a corrupt and disorganized ruling class, and a defeated and discredited army. Hundreds of Iranians joined the Tudeh, seeking personal identification with an organization which was anti-imperialistic and which had ready answers for their basic aspirations. In November 1941, the Provisional Committee of Fifteen began publishing a journal called *Siasat* ("Politics"), by means of which the party organization was to be spread throughout the nation.[9]

The party's first provisional conference was held in Tehran in June 1942. At this meeting, attended by 120 delegates representing intellectuals, professionals, and workers, the groundwork for forming a mass party was devised. The party also made concrete demands on the government. These included formation of a democratic government representing the broad strata of the population; implementation of the constitutional provisions related to political liberties and human rights; abolition of Reza Shah's antidemocratic laws, particularly the June 1931 Act prohibiting Communist and antimonarchial parties; distribution of Reza Shah's properties, state lands, and other large holdings among the peasants; acceptance of an eight-hour work day, recognition of trade unions and the right of collective bargaining; and the granting of politcal and social rights to women.[10]

The journal *Siasat* was suspended by the conference, since its editor was no longer a member of the party. It was then decided to publish the newspaper *Rahbar* "The Leader" as the official organ of the party. Through another publication, *Mardom* "The People," the party sought to combat Fascism, which it believed to have penetrated the ruling class and a considerable segment of the literate middle class.[11]

To broaden the base of the party, early in 1943 Tudeh leaders established contact with the editors of more than twenty publications of a liberal-democratic bent with the idea of framing a uniform editorial policy—a "Freedom Front" dedicated to two basic struggles: (1) opposition to the restoration of dictatorship and (2) opposition to Fascism.[12] The idea quickly caught on, and the "Freedom Front" spread to the major provinces, embracing a total of forty-four newspapers.[13]

Under the direction of veteran trade union organizers, unions were set up in Tehran, Meshed, Isfahan, and Tabriz. By 1944, the party had gathered most of the trade unions into a new organization, the Central United Council, headed by Reza Rusta.[14]

The Council's aim was to better the conditions of the workers, notably in the areas of wages, health, and education. In the early stages the growth in the ranks of the Council was impressive, and at the end of the first year it claimed 150 thousand members. It must be noted that in the North the presence of Russian troops was instrumental in this expansion. For example, in many factories in that region the workers were forced to join the Council.[15]

From 1 August to 12 August 1944 the first Tudeh Party Congress met in Tehran. One hundred sixty-four delegates, from a total membership of 25 thousand, assembled to deal with the party statutes, programs, and organization. Each delegate, representing about 150 members, had been elected in a designated section by a local conference of the party. In class composition, seventy five percent came from labor*; twenty three percent represented the intelligentsia; and two percent the peasantry.[16]

Decisions had to be made on both the party's ideological makeup and its tactical position. There was diversity and dissension within the Congress concerning these issues and others, such as the organizational structure of the party.

Khalil Maleki, one of the theoreticians of the party, led the attack on the Tudeh leadership by criticizing their decision to participate in the parliamentary elections of the Fourteenth Majlis. He accused the party leaders of political opportunism and argued that such cooperation had enhanced the prestige of a weak and corrupt regime. Maleki pressed for a more radical and revolutionary approach in the struggle to protect the rights of the workers and peasants against the corrupt ruling classes.[17]

The leadership acknowledged the validity of some of the criticism but retorted that if the Tudeh Party was to strengthen its base and attract the masses and the middle class to its cause, it became imperative to participate in the parliamentary elections. They further explained that more radical tactics during the early stages would have resulted in the disintegration of the United Front and the outlawing and destruction of the party.

The Congress approved the principle of collective leader-

---

* This percentage only represents their aspirations, and is misleading. The Tudeh party included many groups as part of the labor force, who are classified differently by Western statistical experts.

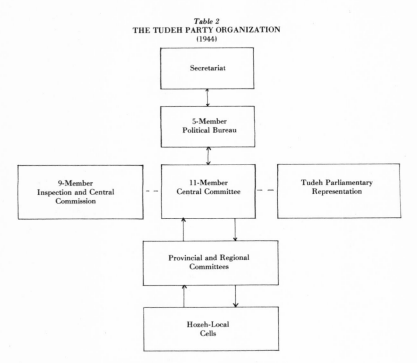

Table 2
THE TUDEH PARTY ORGANIZATION
(1944)

Source: Official Publication of the Government of Iran, *Evolution of Communism in Iran from Shahrivar 1320, September 1941 to Farvardin 1336, April, 1957* (Tehran: 1959)

ship. Its new organizational structure called for the election of three general secretaries. In addition, eleven members were to be elected to the Central Committee and nine others were to constitute the Inspection and Control Commission. Another major organ was the Political Bureau, whose five members were to be chosen from among the ranks of the Central Committee. The three general secretaries were to be selected from the Political Bureau. (See table 2)

The Central Committee wielded the most authority over party organization and activity, but shared some of its power with the independently elected Inspection and Control Commission. A major role of that commission was to work out the details for a more selective and stricter recruiting procedure. The main functions of the Political Bureau and the general secretaries were supervision and administration of the party organization and execution of the decisions of the Central Committee.[18]

The Congress supported the leadership in its decision to participate in the parliamentary elections and to establish a united front against Fascism. It mandated the newly elected Central Committee to resist any imperialistic threats to the territorial integrity, political independence, or security of Iran.[19]

The approved party statute emphasized the principle of "democratic centralism" by means of the following requirements: (a) strict party discipline with the minority obeying and executing the decisions of the majority; (b) the obligation of party members and lower organs to execute the directives of the higher organs; (c) the right of the leadership to appoint responsible individuals to the executive organs of the party; (d) the right of the leadership to give assignments to party members who were to obey and execute all directives; (e) the punishing of those members who were lax or negligent in the execution of party directives.[20]

The Tudeh leaders borrowed the term "democratic centralism" from Lenin's vocabulary, and their intention was to exer-

cise discipline and central control over the membership rather
than emphasizing democratic principles. It was left to the
Inspection and Control Commission to put into effects rules
and regulations concerning the membership and to see to it
that the decisions and orders of the leading party organs were
implemented.

The Party Congress of 1944 marked the party's transformation from what was originally an "anti-Fascist" group to
a mass political organization working for basic social and
political change.

As for the Tudeh newspapers, they continuously attacked
the Iranian establishment as "Fascist," "enemy of freedom
and democracy," and "stooge of the imperialists." The
following excerpt from the newspaper *Rahbar* was typical:

> Our fight against the ruling class will be relentless and
> continuous. This corrupt and decayed structure must be
> destroyed. Any government which fights our movement is
> Fascist and must be eliminated. Any group which hinders
> real cooperation between Iran and the Soviet Union is the
> lackey of British imperialism and the foe of the Iranian
> people. The present ruling groups are holdovers of the Reza
> Shah regime and cronies of the imperialist embassies. The
> masses should unite to bring about their liquidation.[21]

The Tudeh naturally became strongest in the northern zone
where Soviet troops were in occupation and where the Tudeh
hierarchy was more powerful and influential than the officials
of the central government. No other party was allowed to exist
and the Soviets made it clear that no government officials
would be given permission to function in the north unless they
were members or supporters of the Tudeh party. The
Russians also gave financial aid to the party. Important
branches were also formed in the industrial center of Isfahan
and in the Anglo-Iranian Oil Company's area in the southwest, as well as in provincial towns like Meshed, Kermanshah, and Hamadan.[22]

In short, in these early years the party began to develop

branches and front organizations but neglected to organize and recruit the peasantry. Not until later did it send agents to the villages to talk to the peasants and to assemble the required documents for frontal assault on the landowners, state lands, and the land system, all based on the exploitation of the peasants.

The Role of the Fourteenth Majlis

The Fourteenth Majlis began its deliberations in February 1944, while Iran was occupied by troops of the Soviet Union, England, and the United States. At that time the agricultural and industrial production of the country was in the hands of the Allied Forces, and the Trans-Iranian Railroad could be used only for the transportation of Lend-Lease goods to the Soviet Union. Famine and disease were widespread. In addition, American companies were pressing the Iranian Government for oil concessions in the southeast while the Russians asked for oil grants in the northern provinces.

The nation needed statesmen and qualified deputies to lead and unite the country, resist foreign pressure and influence, reestablish constitutional democracy, eliminate corruption, and defend the interests of the people. But, from its inception, the Fourteenth Majlis was paralyzed and could not cope with the many pressures which were leading the country into chaos and anarchy.[23]

A source of considerable concern was the rigging of the Majlis elections by Ali Soheili, the prime minister, and Seyd Mohammed Tadayon, the interior minister. With the exception of deputies from Tehran and some of the provinces, the majority of the members were not elected by the electorate and thus did not represent the people. In some areas members had been elected with the help of the Russians or the British, in others through the direct interference of Soheili's government. Since the elections were not free, the majority of the deputies did not enjoy the confidence of the populace.

There was little party organization in the Fourteenth Majlis. About fifty percent of the old deputies had survived, but among the new ones were several leading personalities such as Dr. Mohammed Mussadeq,* who was elected from Tehran without the aid of any party backing.

* Mussadeq was born in 1879. His father was a minister of the Court and his maternal uncle, a prince. He obtained his diploma at the Ecole des Sciences Politiques in Paris, and shortly after began working at the Ministry of Finance, where he remained for ten years. In good elite fashion he returned to Europe for advanced studies, first at the University of Liege in Belgium, then at the University of Neuchatel in Switzerland. Equipped with a Doctorate of Jurisprudence, he returned to Iran and promptly became involved in politics.

In 1915 Dr. Mussadeq was elected to the Third Majlis. There he served on a committee concerned with the reorganization of the Ministry of Finance. In 1921 he was appointed governor-general of Fars. He also served as minister of finance. Later he was appointed governor-general of Azerbaijan and, in 1923, minister of foreign affairs.

He was elected as a deputy from Tehran to the Fifth Majlis which convened in January 1924. In the debate over the termination of the Qajar Dynasty and the question of entrusting the government to Reza Khan, pending the calling of a constituent assembly, Dr. Mussadeq made a lengthy speech in which he stated that the fundamental laws of the country had to be preserved. He insisted that they would be destroyed if the Qajars were removed and Reza Khan put into their place. He was re-elected to the Sixth Majlis and opposed Reza Shah at every turn. Reza Shah saw to it that he was not elected to the Seventh Majlis.

Around 1930, upon the order of Reza Shah, Mussadeq was banished from Tehran to exile in Semnan and then in Ahmadabad, an agricultural village owned by his family. He was also imprisoned by Reza Shah. After Reza Shah was forced into exile, Dr. Mussadeq, in 1944, was elected deputy from Tehran to the Fourteenth Majlis where he was viewed by many as a man of principle who had endured the hostility of Reza Shah and survived. He soon became the leader of the Iranian Nationalist Movement and opposed the granting of oil concessions in the northern provinces to the Soviet Union.

Dr. Mussadeq was elected to the Sixteenth Majlis as the leader of the National Front. In the Majlis he led the struggle for the nationalization of the Anglo-Iranian Oil Company. In April 1951, the Majlis and the Senate passed the bill nationalizing the oil industry. On 30 April 1951, Mussadeq was elected Prime Minister by a large majority of the Majlis. One day later, on 1 May, nationalization went into effect and all of the British administrators and technicians were asked to leave Iran. Consequently, the British government did all it could to undermine the support of the government headed by Premier Mussadeq.

Mussadeq successfully resisted all pressures including the complaint filed by England against Iran with the United Nations Security Council. In the summer of 1952, Mussadeq defended Iran against the British complaint brought before the International Court of Justice. Mussadeq said the World Court had no jurisdiction since nationalization was purely an internal act. On 22 July 1952, the International Court of Justice, adopting the Iranian viewpoint, decided it was without jurisdiction in the oil dispute.

The presence of the British and the Russians in the occupied areas brought into existence factions that either favored the British or supported the Soviet Union. The Tudeh Party elected nine members[24] to the Majlis. With the notable exception of Taqi Fadakar, who was elected from Isfahan in the British zone, all the others came from the Soviet-controlled northern provinces.

Another group of twenty-five deputies, called the *Mehan* ("Fatherland") faction, favored the British and opposed the Tudeh vehemently. They were elected mainly from the southern provinces which were under British control. Strongly anti-Communist, they represented the interests of landowners and the big business sector. They also supported a strong military establishment and a no-compromise policy toward the Soviet Union.

The Center was represented by three groups, *Ittihad-i-Melli* "National Union", *Azadi* "Liberty", and *Mardom* "People". Basically middle class and independent, they tried to preserve a nonaligned approach in the debates between the Right and the Left. Elected mainly from Tehran and the central provinces, they favored a neutral prime minister—who would move to win the confidence of the Soviet Union. Some were landowners, but the majority were university professors, businessmen, and journalists. On major issues they followed Dr. Mussadeq's lead, although Mussadeq was an independent and did not belong to any parliamentary faction.

The decision greatly strengthened Mussadeq's position and he had scored another victory in his chain of many triumphs. Meanwhile, economic boycotts and intrigues against Iran continued and the United States decided to take an active role in the future developments in Iran. The Eisenhower administration, with the encouragement of the British, started to use the Shah as a pawn in the plot against Mussadeq and his popular national government. The CIA was given the task of organizing the plot to overthrow the Mussadeq government. On 19 August 1953, the CIA, conspiring with the Shah's sister Ashraf and General Fazlollah Zahedi, conducted a *coup d'état* in Tehran that resulted in the overthrow of the Mussadeq government and the return of the Shah who three days before had fled to Rome.

Mussadeq was sentenced to three years of imprisonment and after serving his sentence, he was banished by the Shah to his village outside of Tehran, where he died in March, 1967.

Table 3
THE STRUCTURE OF THE FOURTEENTH MAJLIS

| TUDEH PARTY 9% | - - - | CONFLICT | - - - | MEHAN [Fatherland] 19% |

14th MAJLIS

MARDOM [People] 8%

INDEPENDENT 35%

AZADI [Liberty] 16%

ITTIHAD-I-MELLI [National Union]

Source: Hussein Kay Ostovan, *Siasat-i-Movazeneh-manfiey, Dar Majlis Chardahom* [Establishment of a negative equilibrium in the 14th Majlis] (Tehran: Majlis Publishing Press, 1949).

A large independent group, mostly left-of-center, represented the professionals and the landowners of the north. They were an important faction and on many issues, by means of their abstentions, tried not to alienate the Soviet Union. During the tenure of the Fourteenth Majlis their lack of support on the different votes of confidence resulted in the fall of seven governments.[25]

According to Dr. Nasrollah S. Fatemi, "A major internal friction developed during the procedural debate over the credentials of Seyyd Zia ud-Din Tabatabai.* The Tudeh Party united with the progressive and anti-British elements to oppose the seating of Seyyd Zia. Dr. Mohammed Mussadeq led this left-of-center coalition."[26]

Dr. Mussadeq argued that since Seyyd Zia had been responsible for the 1921 *coup d'état*, which had brought about Reza Shah's dictatorship, and because the change in the dynasty had been supported and backed by the British, Seyyd Zia had to be disqualified as a member of the Majlis. Mussadeq also claimed that the people of Yazd had not been free to choose their deputies and that Seyyd Zia had been elected through the interference of the central government.

Mussadeq further asserted that "Any individual who subverts, or leads an open revolt against the constitutional government or the independence and the territorial integrity of the country, if found guilty, loses his right to seek election to the Majlis."[27]

The Tudeh and the pro-Russian members also opposed Seyyd Zia because of his pro-British and anti-Soviet position

---

*Seyyd Zia ud-Din Tabatabai and Reza Khan had engineered the *coup d'état* of 1921. Seyyd Zia became Premier but later lost favor and was forced into exile in July, 1921. He returned to Iran in 1943. Upon his return he strove to organize a nationalistic, pro-British, anti-Communist party at first called *Vatan* "Fatherland", later renamed *Iradeh Melli* "National Will", which was officially inaugurated in January 1945. He established the newspaper *Raad Emruz* ("The Thunder of Today"), edited by Prince Mozaffar Firouz which was outspoken in its denunciation of the Tudeh and hostile to Soviet penetration of the country. Seyyd Zia was elected Deputy to the Fourteenth Majlis from Yazd, his home town. Interview with Dr. Nasrollah S. Fatemi, former Deputy of the Fourteenth Majlis, New York, 15 March 1969.

and felt that the approval of his credentials would provoke the Russians and cause a deterioration of the relations between the two countries.

The *Mehan* faction and some independent members from Tehran and the southern provinces pointed out that the *coup d'état* had taken place twenty-three years before and that Seyyd Zia had never been charged, tried, or convicted for any complicity in that coup. They also argued that the son of Reza Shah, the dominant figure of the 1921 *coup d'état*, was now King and that it would be unfair to punish Seyyd Zia by depriving him of his seat from Yazd. Furthermore, they felt that the Tudeh's argument was an insult to the sovereignty of the nation, for if pro-Soviet deputies were elected without provoking the British, why would Seyyd Zia's presence in the Majlis be considered a provocation of the Russians?

After heated debate, in March 1944 the majority of the deputies voted to seat Seyyd Zia ud-Din Tabatabai as a member from Yazd.[28] During the debate it had become evident that Seyyd Zia and his supporters would retaliate by challenging the credentials of some of the pro-Soviet deputies. One person they challenged was Jafar Pishevari. Pishevari, a native of Iranian Azerbaijan, who lived in Baku (1904-18), had played a leading role in the short-lived Gilan Republic, returning to Soviet Russia following its collapse in 1921. There he remained until 1936, when, together with a group of refugees who claimed to have been deported by the Soviet Secret Police, he reentered Iran. Released from Iranian custody by the 1941 amnesty, he became the leading instrument of Soviet tactics in Azerbaijan. Editor of the newspaper *Azhir* "Alarm", Jafar Pishevari often attacked the monarchy and the reactionary majority in the Majlis and had repeatedly advocated an armed revolution. He was elected to the Majlis from Tabriz.[29]

According to Dr. Fatemi, "Pishevari went against tradition by taking part in numerous debates before his credentials were approved. In one speech he violently attacked the government and the members of the Majlis, calling upon the exploited workers to overthrow the regime and the decadent Iranian establishment." Said Fatemi, "This attack precipitated much hostility, and even the centrists, who would have voted to seat him, ended up by opposing him."[30]

Opponents charged that Pishevari, as minister of the interior in the Gilan Soviet Republic, had been responsible for much of the bloodshed in the city of Rasht. Evidence was also produced that the Russians had influenced his election from Tabriz.

Supporters of Pishevari, including Dr. Mussadeq, felt that there was no evidence regarding Resht and argued that his election from Tabriz did not differ from that of Seyyd Zia and other members from the occupied zones. Mussadeq also pointed to the inconsistency in the fact that of the nine deputies elected from Tabriz, seven were being accepted and two turned down, though all had been elected under the same electoral process.[31]

Pishevari's credentials were rejected in July 1944, and the Left thus lost an experienced leader at a very critical time. To Nas Rollah Fatemi, "this was probably one of the greatest mistakes of the Fourteenth Majlis. Some members had advised against vendetta, contending that Pishevari inside the Majlis would have been less harmful than outside. They may have been right for if Pishevari had been in the Majlis, he might not have helped precipitate the Azerbaijan insurrection a year later."[32]

The clash over credentials initiated a prolonged rivalry between the forces supporting British diplomacy, led by Seyyd Zia, and the Tudeh Party, in coalition with the progressive, anti-British elements favoring the Soviet Union.

The conflict between the two fronts not only led to instability and numerous changes of government but also dealt a serious blow to Irano-Soviet relations, dashing the hopes of the democratic forces who saw in the Soviet Union a friendly neutral power, ready to help Iran clean its domestic corruption and resist British interference.

An analysis of the Majlis documents indicates that as the Tudeh Party became more dependent on Soviet diplomacy and little more than a Soviet mouthpiece on major issues, the independent non-Communist deputies found it difficult to support the Tudeh, and a third force emerged under the leadership of Dr. Mussadeq.

Kavtaradze and the Oil Crisis

Toward the end of 1944, the three Allied Powers began to anticipate the situation that would arise when the occupation troops were finally withdrawn. The split between East and West was beginning to emerge—in fact, it was in Iran that it first became obvious. From a policy of restraint, the Allies now moved toward a policy of manipulation hardly conducive to political stability in Iran. The Soviets began to consider the Tudeh Party as a possible instrument of policy, and soon the party became identified with Soviet policy in Iran. Russia's open espousal of the Tudeh coincided with the oil crisis that developed in the fall of 1944 when the Soviets demanded oil concessions in the northern provinces.[33]

This situation began to develop in the fall of 1943 when Shell, an Anglo-Dutch company, applied for oil concessions in southeastern Iran. In the spring of 1944 two American companies—Standard-Vacuum and Sinclair—also sent representatives to Tehran and submitted proposals to the government.[34] Iran engaged two American petroleum experts, A. A. Curtis and Herbert Hoover, Jr., to study the proposals of the American companies and prepare a counter proposal for the government.

On 12 August 1944, Dr. Reza Radmanesh, a member of the Tudeh faction in the Majlis, attacked the government of

Premier Mohammed Saed for its secret oil negotiations. He demanded to know why Iran had engaged Americans to advise it on concessions which were being granted to American companies. Expressing the decision of his party, he demanded the immediate dismissal of Curtis and Hoover and went on record vehemently opposed to any oil concessions to a foreign country. Radmanesh warned the government that its action was detrimental to the national interest and threatened impeachment proceedings against Saed.[35] A week later Premier Saed broke a long silence and stated in the Majlis that the government was studying the possibility of granting oil concessions but that the final decision would be up to the Majlis.

In the middle of September, the Soviet Union dispatched Sergei I. Kavtaradze, assistant commissar for foreign affairs, to Tehran. He was warmly received by the Iranians and, after a round of dinners, receptions, and audiences, left for a tour of the northern provinces. Upon his return to Tehran, Kavtaradze met with Premier Saed and submitted a note to the Iranian government chiding it for its negotiations with British and American oil companies without considering their detrimental effect on the interests of the Soviet Union. The note proposed that:

1. The Soviet Union be granted oil concessions in the area consisting of the Provinces of Azerbaijan, Gilan, Mazanderan, Astrabad, and Khorasan.

2. The duration of the concession be seventy-five years.

3. The Soviet government would start, within five years, exploratory work in the whole area. After a geological survey of the region, the Soviet government would redefine the concession area and notify the Iranian government of the regions in which oil resources were assured.

4. The details of the concession regarding royalties, payments to the Iranian government, capital,

management, personnel, purchase of land from individuals, the number of Russian technicians and their relations with the government of Iran, as well as other details should be decided after ratification of the concession by the Majlis.[36]

On 16 October 1944, the Iranian government informed the British, Soviet, and American Embassies that negotiations concerning oil concessions would be postponed until after the end of the war. This announcement led to an intensification of Soviet activities both in the Majlis and in the press. Kavtaradze remarked that the answer was equivalent to a rejection of the Soviet proposal and would tarnish the friendly relations between the two countries.[37]

Premier Saed then disclosed to the Majlis that for months he had been negotiating with Anglo-Dutch Shell, Standard-Vacuum, and Sinclair concerning oil concessions in different areas of Iran, but that the government had concluded that all negotiations were to be deferred until the post-war period.

"The Soviet Mission," Saed added, "was also informed that the Iranian government would like to postpone discussions on oil concessions to the period after the war. But unfortunately some newspapers and political circles have interpreted this decision as an anti-Soviet act. This is not true. Iran has been a strong and loyal ally of the Soviet Union in the prosecution of the war against Nazi Germany and in the future will strive to strengthen this friendship and cooperation between the two governments."[38] Saed's statement was followed by attacks by the Tudeh deputies on the government and the Majlis majority.

On 22 October, the Soviet trade-union newspaper *Trud* launched a sharp attack on the policies of Premier Saed. The article stated "The Iranian government had left unpunished the harmful actions of certain ill-intentioned elements who had disrupted the regular flow of Allied supplies to the Soviet. . .and had not opposed the present intensification of subversive work by pro-Fascist elements in Iran." *Trud* added: "Because of Mr. Saed's policies, Iranian relations with the Soviet Union have become tense and strained."[39]

Quoting from *Shahbaz*, the leftist newspaper, *Trud* went on to assert that reactionaries had set Premier Saed to the task of smashing workers' organizations and democratic organizations and had introduced a bill for the militarization of industry. *Trud* also revealed that many Iranian papers were asking Saed to resign because his leadership was harming the interests of Iran and the Iranian people.[40]

The stage was thus set for an interview with Kavtaradze arranged by a large number of Iranian editors at the Soviet Embassy on 24 October. During this press conference, Kavtaradze stated that proposals for the Soviet concession were guided by a friendly attitude toward Iran and a desire to protect Iran's independence. He said that Premier Saed's refusal had made a very unfavorable impression in Moscow, and that the disloyal and unfriendly position taken by the Premier excluded the possibility of further collaboration with him. Kavtaradze appealed to the Iranian public to pressure the government for a favorable solution of the dispute. He outlined the advantages that Iran could receive if the Soviet concession were approved. First, it would decrease unemployment; second, it would develop Iran's mineral resources; third, it would increase the market for agricultural produce in the areas under concession; and fourth, it would train many Iranians for skilled jobs.

Kavtaradze concluded by appealing to the free press of Iran to inform and enlighten the public and noted that he was pleased that the "majority" of the press in Tehran supported the Soviet position.[41]

Responding to this cue, the newspapers of the Freedom Front launched a denunciation of the Saed government, asserting that Iran would benefit economically from the proposed Russian concession. They insisted that the rejection of the Soviet proposal, particularly in view of the lengthy and secret negotiations for concessions with the Americans and the

British, proved beyond a doubt that Mohammed Saed was the tool of "imperialist reactionaries."

Massive demonstrations against the government broke out in the Soviet Zone, while in Tehran Soviet army trucks carried considerable numbers of Tudeh party members to a demonstration before Majlis. Red Army units helped neutralize the Iranian Army Security Forces at the Tehran rally.[42]

The reversal of Tudeh's position on granting oil concessions to foreign governments and the demonstration before the Majlis with the support of the Soviet forces helped reveal the party as not a disinterested progressive element, but as a tool and instrument of Soviet interests in Iran. The Tudeh, exposed as a pro-Russian party, was isolated and lost its support within the progressive nationalist bloc.[43]

The threatening situation forced Saed to call a press conference. He gave the following reasons why his cabinet refused to negotiate a concession with the Soviet Union:

1. So long as foreign troops were in Iran all concessions would be considered as granted under duress.

2. The economic and political situation of the world was unclear.

3. The government of Iran was waiting for the result of the Anglo-American oil conference in Washington, D.C.

4. Iranian representatives abroad urged that no concessions be granted until the end of the war.[44]

Soviet propaganda intensified. Radio Moscow accused the Iranian government of "pursuing an anti-Soviet policy," but it reminded the audience that "none of the agitators can affect the deep-rooted friendship between the Iranian nation and the Soviet peoples." The Russian broadcast also stated that "all Iranian patriots have expressed their gratitude to the Red Army, and that is why they are disgusted with Saed's government."[45]

Izvestia renewed the attack on Saed's government for its

refusal to grant oil concessions and implied that the Iranian government had favored British and American oil interests. It also pointed to the fact that American troops were present in Iran without any treaty.

In a review of Russia's complaints against Iran's policies, *Izvestia* centered its fire on the late Reza Shah, Premier Mohammed Saed, and the former Premier Seyyd Zia ud-Din Tabatabai. It declared that "reactionaries" were compelling Saed "to pursue a reactionary policy inimical to the Soviet Union." It added that Saed was a puppet of Seyyd Zia and the reactionary cliques behind him, who had nothing in common with real Iranian patriots.

The *Izvestia* article labeled as subterfuge a statement by Seyyd Zia in his newspaper, *Raad Emruz*. Zia claimed that the American ambassador to Iran had written that the decision not to award oil concessions before the end of the war produced neither regret nor vexation in American circles because Iran was an independent state. To *Izvestia* Seyyd Zia's newspaper delicately passed over the question of how the presence of troops of another state on Iranian territory without any treaty was consonant with Iran's sovereignty and independence. The article added that, although Soviet and British troops were in Iran in conformity with the treaty of alliance, the United States forces were in Iran without any treaty.

The *Izvestia* article pointed out that in 1921 Russia had voluntarily and without compensation surrendered the former Russian Oil concession in northern Iran, on condition that it would not subsequently be transferred to foreign states.

The Iranian government had broken that agreement, said *Izvestia*, by granting a concession to Standard Oil Company in the five Northern Provinces in 1926.

In conclusion *Izvestia* charged that "criminal and pro-Fascist elements" had influenced Premier Saed's decision to turn down the Russian oil concessions and his efforts to hinder a rapprochement between the USSR and Iran.[46]

The State Department in Washington, D.C. met this extraordinary contention from an ally by observing acidly that American service troops, and not combat forces, were in Iran to expedite the delivery of Lend-Lease goods to the Soviet Union.[47]

Dr. Mussadeq and the Neutralization of the Major Powers

Kavtaradze remained in Tehran as political tensions rapidly mounted. The Tudeh called for a demonstration on 7 November 1944, to commemorate the anniversary of the Russian revolution. Backed by the Shah, Saed ordered the military governor of Tehran to crack down on the party and squelch its rally. The headquarters of the party were raided by the police and the demonstrators dispersed by force. Soldiers occupied the offices of Tudeh newspapers, and several leaders of the party including Reza Rusta, the head of the Labor Union, were arrested.

This action expedited the fall of the Saed government. On 9 November he resigned, and it was not until 20 November 1944, that the Majlis elected Morteza Qoli Bayat as his successor.

The Russians and the Tudeh Party greeted the new government with reservations. During a debate in the Majlis, the Tudeh deputies pointed out that if Bayat hoped to stay in power, he would have to settle the oil problem. They also called for the dissolution of the anti-Tudeh groups, especially Seyyd Zia's party.

Such were the conditions when, on 2 December 1944, Dr. Mohammed Mussadeq, who had been urged by the majority in the Majlis to form a government following the resignation of Saed but had refused, introduced a bill prohibiting oil negotiations with foreign countries.[48]

Dr. Mussadeq, in a previous speech, had given a detailed review of the operations of the Anglo-Iranian Oil Company and had described how detrimental these had been to Iran. He had cited facts and figures regarding oil production, concession agreements, and revenues received, to prove the tremendous advantage the British had enjoyed over the host country. He had called the current struggle the most important in his life and had suggested that the three powers— England, the United States, and the Soviet Union—were interested in making a permanent arrangement regarding the oil resources of Iran. Dr. Mussadeq also emphasized that it was in the interest of Iran to seek a political equilibrium ". . .that would neutralize the designs of the major power."[49]

In introducing his bill, Dr. Mussadeq told the Majlis that outlawing the negotiation of oil concessions with foreigners during the war would not only stop the partition of the country but would also pave the way for correction of past wrongs.

During the debate Dr. Fereidoun Keshavarz, a member of the Tudeh faction, stated that it was the wish of the nation to grant an oil concession to the Soviet Union so that a "positive equilibrium" could be established in Iran's relations with the Soviet Union and England. Dr. Mussadeq answered that Keshavarz's proposal reminded him of a man who, having lost his right hand, voluntarily cuts off his left to establish a "positive equilibrium" in his body. This was not what the Iranians wanted. Political equilibrium meant preserving Iranian sovereignty over its northern territory, then concentrating on reestablishing control over the southern territory. The best policy for Iran, Mussadeq insisted, was to throw the two powers out and to keep them out forever.[50]

Dr. Mussadeq's bill was approved by the Majlis without any amendments and against the opposition of the Tudeh members. It provided the following:

1. No prime minister, minister, or other member of the government might enter into negotiations for an oil concession with any official or unoffical representatives of any foreign government or representatives of foreign oil companies or anybody else, or sign any pact

or agreement relating to the oil concession which might incur legal obligations for Iran.

2. The prime minister and the ministers could negotiate only government-approved plans for the exploitation of Iranian oil reserves and management of the oil industry and for the sale of oil. The details and the results of the negotiations had to be reported to the Majlis.

3. The penalty for the violation of the law was to be solitary confinement for a period ranging from three to eight years and permanent dismissal from government service.[51]

On 8 December Kavtaradze invited Premier Bayat and a number of Majlis representatives and newspapermen to the Soviet Embassy. Strongly critical of the new law, Kavtaradze felt that its passage would only serve the interests of those who wanted to hinder good relations between Iran and the Soviet Union. He pointed out that since the British oil concession in the South was not touched, the ban on new oil concessions was not logical. He urged the Majlis to reconsider the Soviet proposals which, he said, were favorable to Iran and not imperialistic in intent. Kavtaradze then said that since the relations between the two countries had deteriorated, he had no choice but to leave Iran immediately. The next day he returned to Moscow.[52]

The failure of Kavtaradze's visit alarmed the nation and created an atmosphere of fear and tension in Iran. Clashes between the Tudeh and anti-Communists became frequent. There were Tudeh mass meetings, demonstrations, and riots. In some of these Red Army units took an active part, thereby casting out all doubt as to why the campaign was being waged. Walkouts and sitdown strikes occurred repeatedly in important industrial cities, such as Isfahan, and in the capital, where armed workers actually assumed control of some major factories.[53] Police authorities in Tehran, Isfahan, and Yazd raided the Tudeh headquarters, and religious leaders intensified their anti-Communist propaganda through the country.[54]

The Tudeh deputies, forced to come out openly in favor of the Soviets, found themselves isolated in the Majlis as the only supporters of the oil concession demanded by the Soviet Union. The Russians realized that Iran was not theirs and that the power of the Tudeh was overrated.

Whatever the real motive of the Soviet action, the Iranian people were antagonized by the high-handedness of Kavtaradze. They were also bewildered by his evasiveness, particularly at the 24 October 1944 press conference, which left many questions unanswered. For instance:

1. What were the differences between the Soviet Oil concessions and those of the British and American concessions in the Middle East?

2. What were the economic and social benefits of the concessions to the northern provinces in particular, and the nation in general?

3. The Russian authorities in Iran had contended that all the buildings, plants, and business premises, and employees of the Soviet companies enjoyed diplomatic immunity. If concessions were granted and the Soviet Union sent thousands of technicians, administrators, accountants, and experts to the northern provinces, what then would be the status of the Soviet personnel? Would they also have diplomatic immunity?

4. What was the status of the Soviet corporation? In which currency would the Soviet government pay the Iranian royalties?

5. The most important question: Was Mr. Kavtaradze *negotiating* economic concessions or dictating an order to the Iranian government?

Kavtaradze had dodged the issues with clever generalizations and maintained that economic, financial, legal, and other issues should be discussed after concessions had been granted.[55]

In February 1945, the British and American representatives traveling to the Yalta Conference discussed in advance their attitudes toward the Iranian question. When the representatives of the three Allied Powers met on 8 February, Anthony Eden urged that the Allies refrain from interfering in Iran's internal affairs. It was not a part of British policy, he declared, to prevent the Soviet Union from obtaining oil in northern Iran, since the Soviet Union was a natural consumer of Iranian oil, but he felt that the Allies should not press for oil concessions until their troops had been withdrawn. He recommended, therefore, that they agree to an earlier withdrawal of troops than was provided for in the "Declaration on Iran."

Edward R. Stettinius pointed out that American oil companies had been carrying on negotiations for oil concessions but had ceased their efforts. The United States, he declared, was content to defer the question of oil concessions until the end of the war. The American troops stationed in Iran, Stettinius observed, were there to transport and guard Lend-Lease supplies from the Persian Gulf to the Soviet Union and for no other reason. He supported the British in regard to an early withdrawal of all troops of all nations.

Both Eden and Stettinius agreed that their governments had no objection to Iran's granting oil concessions to the Soviet Union. Although the Allied treaty with Iran called for the withdrawal of troops no later than six months after the end of hostilities, Eden urged that the troops be withdrawn as soon as the supply route was no longer necessary.

V. M. Molotov declared that the question of oil concessions and the withdrawal of troops were two different matters. Molotov said that when the Soviet Union had questioned the Iranian ambassador about the Iranian attitude to a request for concessions, a favorable reply had been received; only then had the Soviet Union opened negotiations. Soon after that the Iranians had adopted the attitude that during the war there would be no concessions. Molotov observed that he could see no reason why negotiations could not be reopened and that, since there were no current negotiations on oil concessions, the whole problem should be left alone to run its course.

As to the question of troop withdrawal, Molotov observed that it had not been before the Soviet government until that moment and would, therefore, take some time to study. In any case, Molotov concluded, it might be advisable to limit the Iranian question to an exchange of views.[56]

Of the various interpretations given at that time to Russian actions in Iran, three deserve special attention. The first held that the exclusion of the Soviet Union from the initial oil discussions between the Iranian government, the United States, and England may have been in part responsible for provoking the Russians. According to this analysis, the main Soviet concern was the exclusion of British and American oil interests from northern Iran and the establishment of a Russian zone of influence in the North to protect the security of the Soviet Union. The Russians had managed, by means of Kavtaradze's mission, to block the attempt of the Saed government to develop oil resources in the North with American capital. They had succeeded also in destroying both the Saed government and the Majlis majority which supported efforts to strengthen ties between Iran and the United States. In the process, they had aroused Iranian fear that Soviet influence in the North was a prelude to eventual absorption.

A second view maintained that the Soviets were seeking to establish a policy of "positive equilibrium" with England. The British had enjoyed extensive privileges in the South, and the Soviets contended that the government of Iran, by granting them oil concessions in the North, would restore balance to a policy which for many years had favored the British.

Dr. Fereidoun Keshavarz, the Tudeh deputy, argued that a policy of equilibrium between the Soviet Union and the United Kingdom would benefit Iran, for the Soviets would check Britain's imperialistic encroachments. In defense of oil concessions to the Soviet Union he stated that a Socialistic state, by its very nature, was noncolonial in character. The Soviet Union, therefore, could not and would not pursue an imperialistic policy, for in a classless society no such exploitations took place. However, Kavtaradze's actions, which reminded many Iranians of the days of the Czarist regime, indicated that the mere label of a classless society did not prevent a nation from behaving like any other major power.

The third interpretation called Soviet belligerence over the oil issue itself an unmistakable example of imperialism. According to this argument, the Soviets really wanted oil and felt that this was the best period for obtaining concessions.

It should be pointed out here that the British were advising the Iranian government to continue the negotiations with the Russians and possibly grant them oil concessions. To some British diplomats in Tehran the Russian demands were a blessing in disguise, for they were hoping that economic concessions to the Soviets in the North would serve as a tacit agreement for the continuation of the English presence in the South.[57]

The British attitude suggested the example of the 1907 partition of Iran to Iranians like Mussadeq, and helped the Majlis to move effectively in thwarting such an eventuality. The Russians consequently decided to move quickly and directly in their own northern zone, setting the stage for the Azerbaijan confrontation while continuing to encourage the Tudeh to remain active and militant elsewhere in the country.

Notes

1. Article 44 of the constitution states: "The King personally has no responsibility and only cabinet ministers in all the affairs of the state are responsible and accountable to the two houses of parliament." Iran, *Qanun-e- Assassi* [Iran, the Constitution], (Tehran: Majlis Press): for an English translation see Amos J. Peaslee, *Constitution of Nations* (Concord: The Rumford Press, 1950), pp. 200-13.

2. For a detailed analysis Ebrahim Khajeh Nouri, *Bazigaran-e Asrae Talaie, Soheili* (The actors of the golden age, Soheil:] (Tehran: Adalat Newspaper Publication, 1320/1941), pp. 451-70.

3. Taghi Erani, *Bashar Az Nazare Maddi* [Man from a materialistic viewpoint] (Tehran: 1945) 4th ed., p. 38; quoted in Sephr Zabih, *The Communist Movement in Iran* (Berkeley:University of California Press, 1966, p. 66 (hereafter cited as *The Communist Movement*).

4. Official Publication of the Government of Iran, *Evolution of Communism in Iran from Shahrivar 1320, September, 1941 to Farvardin 1336*, April 1957 (Tehran: 1959), pp. 62, 72 (hereafter cited as *Evolution of Communism in Iran*).

5. Zabih, *The Communist Movement*, p. 67.

6. Ibid., pp. 67-68.

7. Abdlsamad Kambakhsh, "Nazari Betarikh Hezab Tudeh Iran" [A look at the history of the Tudeh party of Iran], *Donya*, vol. 7, no. 1 (Spring, 1967), pp. 49-50.

8. Iraj Eskandari, "Histoire de Parti Toudeh," *Moyen-Orient*, no. 6 (December, 1949), p. 9; cited in Zabih, *The Communist Movement*, pp. 73-74.

9. Abdolsamad Kambakhsh, "Tashkil Hezab Tudeh Iran" [The structure of the Tudeh party of Iran], *Donya*, vol. 7, no. 3 (autumn 1967), p. 30.

10. Ibid., pp. 33-34.

11. Abdolsamad Kambakhsh, *Nazari Be Jumbesh Kargari Va Communisty Dar Iran* [A glance at the Communist labor Movement in Iran] (Publication of Tudeh Party of Iran, 1972), p. 63 (hereafter cited as *Communist Labor Movement*).

12. Zabih, *The Communist Movement*, p. 78.

13. Kambakhsh, *Communist Labor Movement*, p. 67.

14. *Evolution of Communism in Iran*, p. 255.

15. Ibid., p. 256.

16. Kambakhsh, *Communist Labor Movement*, p. 69.

17. Ibid., p. 74.

18. Ibid., pp. 70-73.

19. Ibid.

20. *Evolution of Communism in Iran*, pp. 165-66.

21. *Rahbar*, 16 December 1944.

22. L. P. Elwell-Sutton, "Political Parties in Iran, 1941-1948," *Middle East Journal*, vol. 3, no. 1 (1949), p. 48.

23. Hussein Kay Ostovan, *Siasat-i-Movazeneh-i-Manfiey Dar Majlis Chardahom* [Establishment of a negative equilibrium in the Fourteenth Majlis] vol. 1. (Tehran: Majlis Publishing Press, 1949), 1:11-13 (hereafter cited as *Negative Equilibrium*).

24. They were Dr. Reza Radmanesh and Dr. Fereidoun Keshavarz (Gilan), Iraq Eskandari and Rahmingoli Khalatbari (Mazanderan), Shahabe Ferdose and Parvin Gonabadi (Khorassan), Abdolsamed Kambaksh (Qazvin), Ardeshir Ovanessian (Christians of the North), and Taqi Fadakar (Isfahan). See *Mozakerat Majlis* [Majlis debates] (Tehran, 1944). It must be noted that Khalatbari was forced to resign from the party and was ousted from its parliamentary faction in September, 1944; see *Rahbar*, 10 September 1944; also *Raad Emruz*, 18 March 1945. The list of elected Tudeh members given by George Lenczowski, *Russia and The West in Iran* (Ithaca, N.Y.: Cornell University Press, 1949), p. 229, is incorrect.

25. Ostovan, *Negative Equilibrium*, pp. 11-17, 291-94.

26. Interviewed with Dr. Nasrollah S. Fatemi, former Deputy of the Fourteenth

Majlis, New York, 15 March 1969.

27. Ostovan, *Negative Equilibrium*, 1:33.

28. At the time of voting, members present were eighty-six. Fifty-seven voted in favor of Seyyd Zia, twenty-eight against, with one abstention; Ibid., p. 81. This case indicated that in the future Mussadeq's left-of-center coalition could expect defeat from a right-center coalition involving similar issues.

29. Ivar Spector, *The Soviet Union and the Muslim World* (Seattle: University of Washington Press, 1959), pp. 195-96.

30. Fatemi (Interview), 15 March 1969.

31. Reza Radmanesh, "Dar Bareh Nehzat 21 Azar" [About the 21st of Azar movement], *Donya*, vol. 6, no. 4 (winter 1966), p. 10.

32. Fatemi (Interview), 15 March 1969.

33. Elwell-Sutton, "Political Parties in Iran, 1941-1948", p. 54.

34. Arthur C. Millspaugh, *Americans in Persia* (Washington: The Brookings Institution), p. 188.

35. *Mozakerat Majlis* [Majlis debates] (Tehran, 12 August 1944), p. 809.

36. Ostovan, *Negative Equilibrium*, 1:159-60, 1:162-63.

37. Ibid.

38. *Mozakerat Majlis* [Majlis debates] (Tehran, 19 October 1944), p. 1,291.

39. *New York Times*, 23 October 1944.

40. Ibid.

41. Ostovan, *Negative Equilibrium*, 1:63.

42. Ibid., pp. 164-65.

43. Ibid., pp. 166-67.

44. *New York Times*, 2 November 1944.

45. *New York Times*, 4 November 1944.

46. *New York Times*, 5 November 1944.

47. Ibid.; *Newsweek*, 13 November 1944, p. 64.

48. Ostovan, *Negative Equilibrium*, 1:184-88.

49. Ibid., pp. 167-82.

50. *Mozakerat Majlis* [Majlis debates] (Tehran, 2 December 1944).

51. *Mozakerat Majlis* [Majlis debates] (Tehran, 3 December 1944), pp. 1,432-56.

52. Ostovan, *Negative Equilibrium*, 1:225-280.

53. Zabih, *The Communist Movement*, pp. 89-90.

54. Ostovan, *Negative Equilibrium*, 1:228.

55. Ostovan, *Negative Equilibrium*, 1:161-65.

56. Edward R. Stettinius, Jr., *Roosevelt and the Russians, The Yalta Conference* (New York: Doubleday and Co., Inc., 1949), pp. 194-95.

57. *Times* (London), 4 November 1944. The article also mentioned that the Soviet Union was following a longstanding British, and a more recent American, example in displaying a lively interest in the Middle Eastern oil supplies, and there was no particular reason why negotiations had to wait until the end of the war.

3   The Azerbaijan Rebellion

At a time when the Iranian response to the Soviet request for oil concessions was a subject of much controversy, Morteza Qoli Bayat, who had replaced Saed as prime minister, sought to pacify both the Russians and the Tudeh party. Bayat believed that through appeasement and friendly overtures he could change the Soviet attitude toward Iran.

The Tudeh members in the Majlis abstained during the vote on Bayat's confirmation; it was the first sign of a limited support from the Tudeh, since they had voted against all other cabinets presented to the Majlis.

Bayat gave the Tudeh freedom to organize demonstrations —some of which led to riots in southern Iran—and suppressed pro-British newspapers. He also replaced anti-Tudeh governors. He tried to persuade the Russians to accept a governor-general for Azerbaijan, but they refused. There is no doubt that Bayat was sincere in his intentions. He was, however, unfortunately naive. In his negotiations with the Russians he was inept, making too many concessions without getting much in return. He underestimated the seriousness of the divisions within the country. He did not receive support from the left and lost the support of the united anti-communist front which had, by this time, decided that there was to be no compromise with either the Tudeh or the Soviets. After having failed to receive a vote of confidence from the Majlis, Bayat resigned on 18 April 1945.[1]

The fall of Bayat led to the polarization of forces in the Majlis. Thirty-five deputies—members of the Tudeh, their sympathizers, and non-Tudeh deputies from the occupied northern areas—wanted Ahmad Qavam, who was also favored by the Russians, as premier.

A majority of the Majlis—seventy members of the Right-Center coalition—opposed Qavam and sought a candidate acceptable to themselves and to the Russians and British as well.

On 3 May, the deputies finally agreed on Ebrahim Hakimi. Seventy-six years old, Hakimi was honest but mediocre, and during the previous sixteen years had not actively participated in the politics of the country. He misjudged conditions and, without consultation or support from the Majlis majority, appointed to his cabinet a group of undistinguished men, mostly close friends and former colleagues. The debate on his government's program took twenty days, during which he was ridiculed, and finally, unable to receive a vote of confidence, he resigned.[2]

The fall of Hakimi marked the beginning of a more radical Soviet approach toward Iran. Russian reaction to the pro-Soviet Bayat and then to the moderate Hakimi showed again that, regardless of who headed the government, no rapprochement was possible as long as the Soviets sought vital political and economic concessions from Iran.

With the fall of Hakimi, there was a marked swing to the Right, while the Left was provoked to a more extreme position. The trend to the Right culminated in the appointment of Sadr-ul Ashraf as prime minister. Sadr was a former minister of justice, and his training in the old school of Moslem theology had made him an uncompromising enemy of Communism and its antireligious stand.

The liberals in the Majlis were suspicious of his conservative views, and the Tudeh party violently opposed him. An opposition of forty, including the Tudeh deputies, boycotted the meetings of the Majlis for four months, thus depriving Sadr's government of the customary vote of confidence. This effective parliamentary obstruction created a delicate constitutional issue about the legality of the new cabinet.[3]

Continuous demonstrations and uprisings raged in Tehran and the northern cities. The border of the Soviet zone was closed and the flow of food and goods from the north was stopped.

Sadr moved quickly to consolidate his position. He dismissed the governor-general of Azerbaijan and appointed as his successor an anti-Communist member of the Majlis, Mehdi Farrukh. The Soviet authorities opposed Farrukh's appointment, and their border guards at Qazvin refused to allow him to proceed to Tabriz.

Sadr placed the organization and direction of the anti-Tudeh forces in the hands of Chief of Staff, General Hassan Arfa, who was accused of using force and terror in an attempt to annihilate the Tudeh party and its branches throughout Iran. Tehran was declared under martial law, and demonstrations were forbidden. Many leftist papers were suppressed.[4]

As the Right and Left moved further and further apart, the Communist movement in Iran returned to a policy of open offensive. Its objectives were to establish a pro-Soviet government, perhaps even a Communist State in Iran. Failing this, it hoped to secure oil concessions in the northern provinces.

Let us now analyze this period in two parts: first, the insurrection in Azerbaijan and the Soviet role; second, the reaction of Hakimi's government to the revolt.

The Insurrection in Azerbaijan and the Soviet Role

Of all the areas in Iran, Azerbaijan provided the most fertile ground for Soviet activities. The most northwesterly province, it was some 35,000 square miles in area. Rich in minerals, it was well watered and fertile, yielding a surplus of wheat, fruits, and wool.

The population in 1945 was roughly two million, comprised of Caucasians, peasants of Turkish stock, Kurds, Armenians, and Nestorian Christians (Assyrians).[5] (See table 4)

The Turkish peasantry was both the largest and the most influential group, numbering around one million. Descendants not of Turks from Turkey but of related tribes, they settled in Anatolia during the great Tartar migrations across Asia. A vigorous, war-like people from whom the Iranian army has long been largely recruited, they were known for their loyalty to the monarchy in the 17th and 18th century. Their language was *Azari-Turkic*, identical to the dialect spoken in Soviet Azerbaijan.

There were also the nomadic Kurdish element moving back and forth across the frontiers of Iran, Iraq, and Turkey. Such

Table 4

BREAKDOWN OF THE DIFFERENT ETHNIC AND LINGUISTIC GROUPS IN AZERBAIJAN, 1945

Peasants of Turkish Stock (*Azari-Turkic*)..............50%
Caucasians (Bilingual, *Farsi*, and *Azari-Turkic*).......40%
Kurds (Kurdish).....................................7%
Armenians and Assyrians (Armenian and Assyrian)......3%

                                                    100%

Source: Mohammed Javad Mashkur, *Nazari Beh Tarikh-e Azerbaijan Va Asar Bastani Va Jmay-yat Shenasi-an* [Reflection on the history of Azerbaijan and its ancient heritage and demographic characteristics] (Tehran: The National Heritage Society of Iran, 1969).

freedom of movement across national borders was a ready sourse of disruption.[6]

Azerbaijan is situated in a strategic area. To the north are the Soviet republics of Azerbaijan and Armenia; to the west, Turkey; to the southwest, Iraq. During the Second World War the province was easily infiltrated when the Red Army dismantled the Iranian-border military, customs, and police posts, extending Soviet Azerbaijan south to include Iranian Azerbaijan. Soviets in Azerbaijan were in a position to cut Turkey off completely from Iran, to open the Turkish back door by exposing the vitally important road running south of Ararat to Erzerum, and to install themselves on the northeastern frontier of Iraq, only 100 miles from the British oil fields at Kirkuk and Mosul.[7]

In Azerbaijan, conditions were ripe for a Soviet-inspired revolt. In contrast to the majority of the people who lived in abject poverty, there was a relatively small class of rich landowners and merchants. To these had been added a small number of contractors who had made enormous profits because of the war.

The workers and peasants had no rights and, in most cases, were at the mercy of the decrees of absentee landlords, corrupt government bureaucrats, and army officers. The landowners used the gendarmerie to enforce their orders against the peasants.[8]

The outspoken minorities of the province held many grievances against the government, most of them dating back to the period of Reza Shah's repressive rule. They protested their proportionately inadequate representation in the governmental system; demanded that the central government accept *Azari-Turkic* as the official language; and pressed for the passage of labor laws, of a law regulating peasant-landlord relations, and of legislation protecting the rights of minorities.

Azerbaijan was a microcosm of conditions existing in Iran. The central government was so weak and indecisive that there could be no agreement on a governor-general for the province, and Premier Sadr was unable to resolve the complaints of the Azerbaijanis. A few contradictory decrees were sent from Tehran to officials in Tabriz, but by this time the Soviets had little difficulty in organizing the populace for revolutionary action. There was also good reason to begin an insurrection in a place where the refusal to seat Pishevari in the Majlis could be exploited to the full.[9]

In Pishevari the Soviets had found not only an experienced revolutionary leader (a former commissar of interior in the short-lived Soviet Republic of Gilan), but a strong-willed Azerbaijani who had spent many years of his life in the Soviet Union.

The Tudeh Party of Azerbaijan started a campaign to stop the oppression of the peasants by pressuring the government in Tehran to instruct the local authorities to discontinue "the practice of tyrannizing the populace."[10]

On 26 August 1945, trouble flared up as members of the Tudeh Party and Pishevari supporters temporarily took control of the city of Tabriz. Under protection of Soviet troops, they captured several government buildings and were able to cut off all communications with Tehran. The Iranian army garrison was confined to its barracks by Soviet occupation forces and then disarmed. Gendarmes sent from Tehran to reinforce the local gendarmerie, which was below strength, were turned back by the Russian forces. This pattern was repeated in the next few weeks throughout Azerbaijan. The Soviets wished to remain in the background as much as possible to avoid antagonizing the local population, but on two occasions they were compelled to come out into the open. Russian troops had to give overt support to the Pishevari forces when the Shahsevan tribe joined the local gendarmerie in resisting the Communist takeover. And the newly formed Azerbaijan army, trained, supplied, and no doubt led by the Soviets, had to be dispatched to the Lake Urumia area, where Shiite Iranians were fighting Assyrian, Armenian, and Kurdish partisans of Pishevari.[11]

When Premier Sadr called an emergency meeting of the Majlis, he was attacked by the Tudeh deputies for declaring martial law and for suppressing a number of leftist newspapers. In the debate that followed, Foreign Minister Anushirvan Sepahbodi stated that the northern part of the country was in chaos and that small bands of agitators were disrupting the orderly function of government. He blamed the situation on the occupying powers, particularly the Soviet Union. Sepahbodi felt that, contrary to the Tripartite Treaty of 29 January 1942,* the Soviet Union had violated Iranian sovereignty and that Red Army soldiers were not only preventing Iranian troops and gendarmes from restoring order, but had also helped the rebels. He further charged that the Iranian government did not have freedom of movement for its army within its own territory and that the allies had forgotten that they were guests in Iran. The foreign minister mentioned that he had instructed the Iranian ambassadors in Moscow and London to urge the governments of the Soviet Union and England to expedite the evacuation of the country.

"Now that the war is over," the Foreign Minister told the Majlis deputies, "Iran should have freedom of action in its

---

* Articles I and V of the Tripartite Treaty provided that the Soviet Union and Great Britain should "jointly and severally undertake to respect the territorial integrity, sovereignty and political independence of Iran" and withdraw their forces from Iranian territory not later than six months following the end of all hostilities (chapter I). Agreement was also reached at the Potsdam Conference (17 July-2 August 1945), that the occupying forces should be immediately withdrawn from Tehran. The evacuation of Tehran was duly reported complete before the end of September. Meanwhile, the United States government had unilaterally announced on 28 August that its troops would be withdrawn from Iran by 1 November except for about two thousand who would temporarily guard military installations. It followed from the date of the armistice with Japan that the subsequent six-month period within which the British and Soviet forces should be withdrawn from Iran would expire on 2 March 1946.

On 19 September, Foreign Secretary Ernest Bevin wrote Molotov expressing Britain's willingness to withdraw her troops, except from the southern oilfield area, by mid-December and suggested that the Soviet Union do the same, except in Azerbaijan. Molotov replied that the Soviet government felt that the withdrawal of troops should be effected within the period laid down in the Tripartite Treaty. See George Kirk, *The Middle East, Survey of International Affairs,* 1945-1950, 3 vols., (London: Oxford University Press, 1954), 3:57-58.

northern territory, and the Soviets should stop their censorship and interference in our internal affairs."[12]

Premier Sadr stated to the Majlis three days later that the situation was very serious, that mobs had attacked and burned shops in many towns of Mazanderan, and that order in the northern part of the country had collapsed. He also reported that the governor of Zanjan had been beaten and that Mehdi Farrukh, the newly-appointed governor-general of Azerbaijan, had been prevented by the Russians from going to Tabriz.[13]

It was the sentiment of the Tudeh leadership in Tehran that its provincial wing in Azerbaijan should be less militant and that the central committee should have control over its actions. But Pishevari felt differently and, on 3 September 1945, he announced the formation of the Democratic Party of Azerbaijan. The provincial branch of the Tudeh Party was officially dissolved and its members incorporated into the new organization. It was decided to form a peasants' militia called *Fedayeens* "Devotees".[14]

Pishevari gives the following account in his memoirs:

> At the time of my return to Tabriz, the only political party was the Tudeh. Unfortunately, its leaders were not only ineffective but had lost their popularity. The other organization called the Freedom Front, composed of many liberals and reformists—although incorruptible and popular—had no power. Therefore, I called a meeting with some of the leaders and after three days of debate, it was decided to form a new party. . .Thus on September 3 we announced the formation of the Democratic Party of Azerbaijan.[15]

According to Dr. Reza Danesh (pseudonym), "Pishevari felt that the Tudeh branch was not revolutionary enough; it had made tactical mistakes and over the years of struggles had failed to produce positive results. He also believed its organization was discredited and saw an immediate need for a new party with its own military branch."[16]

The Democratic Party was administered by a central committee located in the city of Tabriz. Pishevari was named its general secretary. District branches were established and sections were organized in the cities, towns, and villages of Azerbaijan. The smallest unit was the village ward, composed of several people.[17]

The new party quickly presented two basic demands to the central government; freedom to teach *Azari-Turkic* in the schools; and provincial autonomy in the development of economic, cultural, and political life. It also expressed its uncompromising opposition to the Sadr government.[18]

On 19 October, Tudeh deputy Dr. Reza Radmanesh told the Majlis that in regard to these demands, the Azerbaijan Democrats had lost all faith in the Tehran government. They looked upon Sadr's government as a continuation of Reza Shah's oppressive rule. Their taxes were spent in Tehran, and the government officials working in Azerbaijan came from the other provinces. Radmanesh stated that the people desired their own legislature, their own governor-general, their own mayor, and control over their system of education and future development.

Radmanesh concluded by stating that the new party was not controlled by the Soviet government, but that it considered the Soviets allies and protectors of the liberal elements in Iran. The Soviet Union, he said, could not remain indifferent to the intrigues and the conspiracies of the ruling circles who, in coalition with foreign governments, were threatening the safety and stability of Soviet Azerbaijan.[19]

Sadr resigned on 21 October 1945, and the Majlis again called on Hakimi to form a government. Hoping to appease the Russians, Hakimi appointed Bayat, the former prime minister, as Azerbaijan's new governor-general. The Soviets consented.[20]

Events moved rapidly, and on 16 November all the elements who had rallied to the Democratic Party came out in open rebellion, cutting off all communications between Tabriz and Tehran and seizing—during the next night—the town and railway junction of Mianeh.[21]

On November 18, an Iranian government spokesman reported that a revolution had broken out in Azerbaijan and that the insurgents had slain at least seven government officials and soldiers. The spokesman added that Russian trucks were distributing weapons to rebels identified as part of the 100 thousand rifles and one thousand machine guns confiscated from the Iranian government by the Red Army when Soviet and British troops occupied the country in 1941.

The spokesman said that the governor of Zanjan telephoned the previous day to report that the rebels had attacked Mianeh and, after heavy fighting, had captured the town and the railroad station.

A merchant arriving in Tehran from Tabriz reported that the rebels had seized Ahar, fifty miles northeast of Tabriz; Sarab, seventy miles east; and Maragheh as well as Mianeh. He asserted that the rebel forces consisted mainly of Armenians, who had migrated to Iran from the Caucasus, and Red Army soldiers, from the Caspian seaport of Baku and who were clad as civilians. The traveler said that the Iranian garrisons at Tabriz, Ardebil (115 miles east of the capital), Rezaieh, and Astara were completely isolated.[22] A relief column, dispatched by the Iranian government to aid the beleaguered garrisons in Azerbaijan, was halted near Qazvin by a Soviet military force whose commander threatened to open fire if it moved further.[23]

An *Izvestia* editorial informed readers that the Democratic Party of Azerbaijan was a spontaneous people's movement established to ensure elementary democratic rights in that province. It reported that the party had met fierce resistance from reactionary, antidemocratic forces who saw in the movement a threat to their domination and privileges, and also that armed assaults had been made in certain districts upon party members by gendarmes and groups organized by reactionary landowners.

Izvestia charged that British reports of Russian intervention in Iran were designed only to divert attention from Palestine and the uprisings in Egypt. "All sorts of scandalous rumors are being spread abroad about Russian lorries providing machine guns and rifles to the Iranian population," the editorial continued, "and many other tales are told all with the aim of concealing the real nature of the Democratic movement in northern Iran and placing responsibility for the incidents on the Russians."[24]

On 20 and 21 November the Democratic Party held an "All-Peoples Grand National Assembly" in Tabriz, with 744 delegates representing 150 thousand inhabitants from all over the province. The delegates unanimously agreed to telegraph the following demands to the Shah, Prime Minister Hakimi, and the speaker of the Majlis:

1. The right to determine the destiny of the people of the province, who possessed a distinctive history, language, and national characteristics.
2. The right of national self-determination without endangering the national sovereignty of Iran.
3. The support of Iran's constitution via representation in the Majlis and payment of a just share of taxes.
4. The freedom to manage domestic affairs within the framework of Iran's sovereignty.
5. The right to elect a provincial Majlis and to form an autonomous government from its membership.
6. The adoption of *Azari-Turkic* as the official language.
7. The threat to fight to the last man if force should be used by the government in Tehran against the movement.
8. An appeal to the democratic nations of the world to help Azerbaijan according to the Atlantic Charter.[25]

The Government's Reaction to the Revolt

On 22 November 1945, the Iranian government dispatched a note to the Soviet Foreign Ministry stating that while

Iranian troops were being halted by the Soviet soldiers, out-siders from the Soviet side of the border were gradually arriving in Zanjan—ostensibly for the purpose of creating troubles similar to those prevailing in Tabriz and other cities of Azerbaijan.[26]

The United States government suggested in a note to the Soviet Union on 24 November that immediate steps be taken to complete the withdrawal of all Allied Forces from Iran by 1 January 1946. The note suggested that those Soviet com-manders who had turned back the Iranian forces in the areas concerned might have been acting without the sanction of the Soviet government, and had "assumed" that the Soviet government was issuing instructions to them in keeping with the Declaration on Iranian Sovereignty signed by the Allies at the Tehran Conference in 1943.[27]

The New York Times of 26 November, quoting diplomatic sources, reported that Foreign Commissar Molotov and Iranian Ambassador Madjid Ahy had engaged in full and frank discussions on the situation in Azerbaijan, and that Mr. Molotov had given assurances that Russia would respect Iranian sovereignty.

Mr. Molotov was said to have expressed surprise at reports that Red Army troops in Azerbaijan had refused free passage to Iranian forces. He had told the envoy that Russia had no intention or desire to interfere with legitimate movements of Iranian troops.

The Soviet government replied on 29 November that the communication of the United States concerning armed up-risings in northern Iran did not correspond to reality. Besides declining the request of the United States for withdrawal of all foreign troops from Iran, the note placed responsibility for the "undesirable incidents" in northern Iran on "reactionary ele-ments which have opposed the extension of national rights to the population of northern Iran." The Soviet note also claimed that "as far as the Soviet military command is con-cerned, it has not hindered and is not hindering, the move-

ments of the Iranian military forces and the gendarme police units which are in the districts of northern Iran."
Furthermore, the message stated:

> The Soviet Government opposed the dispatch of new Iranian troops to northern districts of Iran and informed the Iranian Government that the dispatch of further Iranian forces to northern Iran could cause not the cessation, but the increase, of disorders and likewise bloodshed, which would compel the Soviet Government to introduce into Iran further forces of its own for the purpose of preserving order and of insuring the security of the Soviet garrison.

The note concluded with the observation that since the Soviet government saw no grounds for renewed consideration of the time limit for the removal of its forces, it was not able to comply with the request of the United States government.[28]

While the maneuvering was in progress, Mohammed Sadeq Tabatabai, the speaker of the Majlis, delivered the following statement to the deputies: "Because of the seriousness of the situation, the Majlis over many meetings has conducted no other business except to consider the problems of Azerbaijan." he expressed the wish that Hakimi and his government would be able to convince the Soviet Union of their sincere desire for cooperation, and of their expectation that Russia would respect the territorial integrity and sovereignty of Iran. Tabatabai also appealed to the Iranian public to stay calm and not take steps to jeopardize Iran's relations with the Soviet Union.[29]

Dr. Djalal Abdoh, the deputy from Tehran, charged that the Russian answer was illogical and disappointing since the troops of a small nation could never be a threat to the Soviet Union. He questioned the support claimed by the Democratic Party of Azerbaijan, charging that the rebel ranks had been covertly swelled with large numbers of *muhajirs* "refugees" from Soviet Azerbaijan, many of whom had been imported to add strength to the military arm of the rebellion. He said, however, that according to his sources, more than one thousand men from the indigenous population had joined Pishevari.

Abdoh observed that the Azerbaijan movement had been brought on by the failures of the central government and the many years of Reza Shah's dictatorship. "I agree with their assumptions," he told the cheering deputies:

> The people of Azerbaijan are dissatisfied with conditions in the country but let me also remind you that few will revolt against the central government under the banner of a foreign power. . .they have sent a telegram to the Shah and the Majlis, stating they are not a separatist movement but seek autonomy within the sovereignty of Iran, provided that the central government will leave them alone. It becomes separatism when they call themselves—a nation of Azerbaijan. They write about the language of Azerbaijan, its culture and customs. This is not correct. The history of Iran and Azerbaijan during the last three thousand years has been the same—we are all one nation and that is Iran. For an example, the present Premier, Hakimi, is from Azerbaijan. Let me emphasize that what Pishevari is asking for is the disintegration of Iran. . .the government has the power to crush this rebellion but unfortunately Russian troops have stopped the Iranian forces from entering the province. How can the Government of the Soviet Union defend this action which is contrary to the spirit of the Atlantic Charter, the Tripartite Treaty, the Tehran Declaration and the Charter of the United Nations? I appeal to the Soviet Union to withdraw its troops and let Iran settle its own internal affairs.[30]

The Democratic Party held general elections for an Azerbaijan Majlis from 3 to 8 December. While the elections were in progress, Morteza Qoli Bayat, who had been appointed governor-general of Azerbaijan at the beginning of Premier Hakimi's term, arrived in Tabriz to start negotiations with Pishevari. Bayat was completely ignored on his arrival and no one representing the Democratic Party met with him.

Bayat issued a communique addressed to the people of the province. Conceding that during the previous twenty years the inhabitants had suffered from oppression, lack of proper education, health facilities, and adequate land reform, he called upon the Democratic Party to start negotiating with him.[31] On 9 December the Hakimi government announced the formation of a council of five elder statesmen to study the implications of the revolt and to enunciate a policy for the nation. The council included two former premiers, Ahmad Qavam and Ali Mansur.[32]

Although Bayat eventually met with Pishevari, little was achieved, and on 12 December Bayat returned to Tehran.[33] Members of the newly elected Azerbaijan Majlis met in Tabriz on the same day to proclaim the Autonomous Republic of Azerbaijan. They elected Shabastari as speaker and Jafar Pishevari as prime minister.

The Structure of the Azerbaijan Republic

Although the new regime avoided outright separation from Iran, its administration, army, and police system were organized in the Soviet image. *Azari-Turkic*, and not *Farsi*, was declared the official language. A new flag was designed, and the Iranian national anthem was abolished. Tabriz became the capital of the state. Azerbaijan's legislature was unicameral and composed of the membership from a single party.

As prime minister, Pishevari* headed a government whose principal leaders had been mostly born or trained in the Soviet Union: Dr. Salamollah Javid, a veteran Communist, minister of interior; General Jafar Kavian, a Communist from Soviet Azerbaijan, minister of war; Dr. H. Mahtash, minister of agriculture; Mohammed Biriya, educated in the Soviet Union, minister of education; Dr. Ourangi, minister of health; Gholam Reza Elhami, born in Turkey and educated

* Pishevari was also minister of labor.

in Moscow, minister of finance; Youssef Azima, minister of justice; J. Kabiri, minister of post, telegraph and telephone; and Reza Rasouli, minister of commerce and economy. Pishevari maintained that the purpose of the movement was not separatism but autonomy; therefore, no minister was appointed for foreign affairs. In addition, General Gholam Yahya Daneshiyan, a native of Georgia who spoke no Persian, was put in charge of the *Fedayeen*.

The judiciary included the supreme court, district courts, and courts of appeal. All of the judges were appointed and could be dismissed by the minister of justice.[34]

Red Army uniforms became the uniform of the People's Army of Azerbaijan, and Russian officers started to train the new forces. Civilian supremacy was assured by the appointment of a political officer to assist the military commander of each unit. Most decisions were made by the political commissar. The party also established several academies for the training of army and police officers. The Democratic Party increased the salaries of all officers by twenty percent.[35]

The new military academy, at the end of the first year, graduated 228 officers whose socioeconomic background was lower middle class. Thirty high-ranking officers from different parts of Iran defected from the central government and came to Tabriz to join the new Democratic army. The total number of officers was 870, 6 of whom were generals.[36]

Most of the arms and munitions of the new army came from the garrisons of the central government, which had surrendered to Pishevari. The Soviet Union assisted with some light arms but supplied no tanks or heavy armaments.[37]

The soldiers were mostly volunteers from the peasantry and the ranks of unemployed workers. The Democratic Party gave highest priority to the political education of the illiterate soldiers, who were told they were part of a national army established for the purpose of liberating the oppressed people of Iran. The many examples of corruption and cruelty of Reza

Shah's officers in Azerbaijan were brought to the attention of the recruits.[38]

Most of the people of Azerbaijan enthusiastically supported Pishevari and the army, and the new Majlis unanimously approved the program of the government. The most important parts of the program were: immediate elections for town councils; the consolidation and strengthening of Azerbaijani autonomy; the introduction of *Azari-Turkic* in all schools; universal free education for children and a continuous struggle to end illiteracy; the develpment of industry and trade; the distribution of lands belonging to reactionary landowners who had fled the province; and the protection of the rights of all citizens, including the minorities.[39]

The spread of the revolutionary virus led to the establishment of a Kurdish People's Republic in western Azerbaijan on 15 December 1945, under the presidency of the veteran Kurdish leader Qazi Mohammad.[40]

On 16 December it was announced in Tehran that General Darakhshani had surrendered the Iranian army garrison in Tabriz to the *Fedayeens* backed by Red Army troops. The commander of the garrison had been ordered by the central government to fight to the last man, but Darakhshani had decided that resisting the Soviets would have been impossible and foolish. The town of Rezaieh was also occupied by the *Fedayeen* and the Red Army Forces and its garrison disarmed and disbanded. The officers and men who surrendered were given the choice of taking an oath to the Pishevari Government or of leaving for Tehran. Many chose the latter.[41]

On the same day the Tudeh newspaper *Mardom*, published in Tehran, stressed the blessings which revolution and Communism would bring to the intellectuals, workers, junior officers, soldiers, and peasants, pointing out that a democratic, free Iran would become the magnet for all the colonial peoples of the Middle East.

Premier Hakimi told the Majlis on 17 December that he

had asked to be received in Moscow to discuss the issues raised by the revolt in Azerbaijan directly with the Soviet authorities. Unfortunately, because of the meeting of the Allied Foreign Ministers in Moscow, the trip was not possible. Hakimi also said that the situation in Azerbaijan had deteriorated but that all necessary steps would be taken to bring the province under the control of the central government. Hakimi then told the cheering deputies that the allied forces should be withdrawn from Iran immediately and that he was considering submitting the Azerbaijan dispute to the Security Council of the United Nations.[42]

The next day Dr. Mohammed Mussadeq declared that Iran should have followed a foreign policy of nonalignment. He told the deputies that Reza Shah's anti-Soviet, pro-British foreign policy had been disastrous for the nation and that Hakimi, instead of reversing that trend to one of neutrality, had continued the bankrupt diplomacy of the past.

Mussadeq stated that he was not opposed to needed reforms in Azerbaijan but felt that change should come by constitutional means and not by revolution or force. He again mentioned the immediate need for drastic internal reforms and criticized Hakimi for his failure to indicate the necessary measures.[43]

"Iran needs a just and honest government:" said Mussadeq, "one which is able to meet the aspirations of the people. The people of Azerbaijan have always fought for the glory and independence of Iran. Instead of threatening them with war and violence, the central government, through negotiations and vigorous action, should move to eliminate the causes of their discontent. The country is ripe for a revolution and Hakimi is impotent. Under the circumstances, he should resign."[44]

At the opening of the Moscow Conference of Foreign Ministers on 19 December 1945 James Byrnes, the American secretary of state, said in his first meeting with Stalin that the

United States was concerned about the events in Iran because of the pledge Roosevelt, Stalin, and Churchill had made at Tehran in 1943. He reminded Stalin that in that pledge the three leaders declared that they were "as one with the government of Iran in their desire for the maintenance of the independence, sovereignty and territorial integrity of Iran." Secretary Byrnes told Stalin that developments within Iran prior to the Moscow meeting indicated that the pledge was in danger of being broken. The Iranian government had protested when the fifteen hundred troops dispatched to the province of Azerbaijan to quell what the Iranians said was an insurrection encouraged by foreign sources had been stopped *en route* and turned back by the Red Army. The Iranian government had thereupon asked for the withdrawal of all foreign troops. The United States government had promptly issued an order to the remaining American troops to evacuate Iran, and the State Department had sent a message to the Soviet Union and the United Kingdom urging that they take similar action.

The Iranian protest was still pending when Byrnes told Stalin that, unless the Allies fulfilled the Tehran Declaration, Iran would place its complaint before the forthcoming meeting of the United Nations. As a signatory of the declaration, the United States would feel obliged to support Iran's right to be heard.[45]

Stalin outlined what he termed "the pertinent facts" in the matter: The location of the Baku oil fields in the south of Russia close to the Iranian border created a special problem. These fields had to be safeguarded against any possible hostile action by Iran against the Soviet Union, and no confidence could be placed in the Iranian government. Since the Soviet Union had a right, by treaty, to maintain troops in the north until 15 March, it did not want to withdraw before that date. The decision to evacuate at that time depended upon the conduct of the Iranian government. Stalin maintained that the

Irano-Soviet Treaty of 1921 gave the Soviet Union the right to send troops into northern Iran if there was a possible danger from an outside source.[46]

Byrnes later stated:

> The more I thought about Generalissimo Stalin's excuse for retaining troops in Iran, the less confidence I had in the Soviet position. It was absurd to claim, as he had, that the Red Army of 30,000 well-trained and fully equipped troops must stop the poorly trained and inadequately equipped Iranian force of 1,500 from marching toward Azerbaijan on the public highway because it feared a disturbance would be created. . .And his admission that the question of withdrawal would be examined on the evacuation date showed that our worries about his fulfilling the Tehran Declaration were justified.[47]

At their second meeting, Byrnes told Stalin that he was "seriously disturbed" by the prospect of the Azerbaijan matter being raised at the first meeting of the United Nations. Since the United States would greatly regret having to oppose the Soviet Union in the very first meeting of the United Nations, Byrnes said he hoped that action would be taken in Moscow to forestall that possibility. He added that it was extremely important to the United States that the Big Powers keep their pledges to smaller nations. Stalin was noncommittal.

Ernest Bevin, the British foreign secretary, presented a plan at this same December Conference of foreign Ministers, to be considered as a basis for the settlement of the Iranian case. He proposed that a Three-Power Commission be appointed to go to Iran to seek a solution to the numerous aspects of the problem, to advise the Iranian government on setting up provincial councils, and to supervise the post-war elections.

Molotov's initial response to the plan was favorable, although he put forward several amendments. Bevin accepted all but one, which left in doubt the stipulated date for the withdrawal of troops from Iran (Bevin's contention was that this date had been established by the Tripartite Treaty of 1942 and should not be changed). However, when the ministers met on the afternoon of 26 December it was clear that the Soviet attitude had hardened. Molotov announced that "the Iranian case is not on the agenda and cannot be considered."[48]

Opposition in the Majlis to Bevin's proposal came from the Right as well as the Left. It was called an enlarged edition of the Anglo-Russian Convention of 1907. Dr. Mussadeq told the Majlis that the American and British ambassadors had met secretly with the Shah and Premier Hakimi to ask support for the Power Commission, which would have the responsibility of investigating the situation in Iran in general, and in Azerbaijan in particular. The proposed commission, he pointed out, would also have the power to implement its recommendations.

Mussadeq claimed that the Shah and the Premier had agreed to the proposal, but that the Soviets—after initially approving the idea—had refused to give it their support. Mussadeq further asserted that "when the commission was brought to my attention and after consultations, I notified the Prime Minister that a number of deputies would like to meet with him. He received us at once. Premier Hakimi presented us with a note from the ambassadors. Their recommendation, if accepted by the Shah and the government, would put an end to the sovereignty of Iran and place the nation under a Three-Power mandate."[49] He told Premier Hakimi that under no circumstances would the deputies accept this humiliating recommendation and that they were grateful to the government of the Soviet Union, which had disavowed any complicity in this scheme threatening the territorial integrity of Iran.

Mussadeq declared to the deputies that "this action by the Hakimi government has convinced us that he should resign and be replaced by a premier who would resist foreign pressure and freely negotiate with the Soviet Union."[50] The Hakimi government announced the rejection of the proposal on 10 January 1946.[51]

Iran's Case before the United Nations

Seyyd Hassan Taqizadeh, head of the Iranian Delegation to the General Assembly and the Iranian Ambassador to England, was instructed by Hakimi to refer Iran's complaint to the Security Council.

Taqizadeh asked both Bevin and Byrnes to advise him whether or not he should file his country's complaint against the continued presence of Soviet troops in Iran and against Soviet interference regarding Iranian affairs in the Security Council. Bevin declined the opportunity to give advice. Byrnes told Taqizadeh that he too would hesitate to offer advice since the Security Council was just being organized, had not even adopted rules of procedure, and should have only the most urgent matters placed before it.[52]

Nevertheless, on 19 January 1946 Taqizadeh formally requested that the Security Council, meeting in London, investigate the "interference of the Soviet Union, through the medium of its officials and armed forces, in the internal affairs of Iran," and of a "situation" which was likely to "lead to international friction."[53] It was noticeable that the Iranian delegation had deliberately called the unhappy affair a "situation" and not a "dispute". While determined to establish the authority of its government in the rebellious province, the Iranian delegation evinced no desire to burn all bridges and alienate the Soviet Union. The delegation desired to achieve its policy objective through bilateral negotiations under the supervision of the Security Council. Taqizadeh made it clear that Iran was ready to negotiate "provided that the matter in dispute remains before the Council."[54]

In reply the head of the Soviet delegation, Mr. Andrei Vishinsky, denied the charge of interference, claiming that negotiations between Iran and Russia had been instituted and concluded successfully on 1 December 1945 with an expression of satisfaction by Iran; claimed that the presence of Soviet troops had no relation to the movement for autonomy in Azerbaijan; and opposed consideration of the appeal to the Security Council.[55]

Arriving at its first decision concerning the case on 30 January 1945, the Security Council recommended direct negotiations and requested the parties "to inform the Council of any results achieved in. . .the projected negotiations."[56]

The following were the attitudes of the various factions of the Majlis toward the Azerbaijan rebellion: the Right, uncompromisingly in opposition to it, sought the help of the West and the United Nations Organization to bring pressure on the Soviets to enforce noninterference; the nationalist progressive elements like Dr. Mussadeq and his supporters— acknowledging the long accumulated grievances of the people of Azerbaijan—emphasized appeasement and compromise; the Left-of-Center, which included the majority of the deputies from Azerbaijan, criticized the failure of successive cabinets to reach an understanding with the Soviet Union, and claimed that the government had long neglected the legitimate aspirations of the people; the Tudeh deputies, representing the Radical Left, unconditionally supported the Democratic Party.

With the successful seizure of power in Azerbaijan, the Tudeh representatives in the Majlis became the official voice of the insurrection in Tehran and used every occasion to advance their cause. They argued that because of Iran's proximity to Socialist Russia, it was impossible for her to preserve a feudal regime and resist social progress. The Soviet Union, on the other hand, merely wanted a democratic regime for its neighbor and had repeatedly disavowed any territorial gains in Iran—but, it also could not tolerate an Iranian regime suspicious of its motives.[57]

On 21 January, Premier Hakimi handed his resignation to the Shah, and on 26 January the Majlis, by a vote of fifty-two to fifty-one, elected Ahmad Qavam al-Saltaneh as prime minister.[58] Under Qavam's leadership the Azerbaijan struggle entered its most crucial stage.

Notes

1. Of the 82 members present for the vote on the motion, 36 voted for Bayat, 43 against him, and 3 abstained; see *Mozakerat Majlis* [Majlis debates] (Tehran, 18 April 1945), pp. 247-55; Ibrahim Safa'i, *Nukhust Vaziran* [Prime ministers], (Tehran: Historical Society of Iran, 1970), vol. I, p. 161.

2. Hussein Kay Ostovan, *Siaset-i-Movazeneh-i-Manfiev Dar Majlis Chardahom* [Establishment of a negative equilibrium in the Fourteenth Majlis], vol. 2. (Tehran: Tabin Press, 1951), 2:11, (hereafter cited as *Negative Equilibrium*).

3. Ostovan, *Negative Equilibrium*, 2:30-35.

4. Radmanesh, "Dar Bareh Nehzat 21 Azar" [About the 21st of Azar movement], *Donya*, vol. 6, no. 4 (Winter 1966), p. 10.

5. Mohammed Javad Mashkur, *Nazari Beh Tarikh-e Azerbaijan Va Asar Bastani Va Jmayyat Shenasi-an* [Reflection on the history of Azerbaijan and its ancient heritage and demographic characteristics] (Tehran: The National Heritage Society of Iran, 1969) p. 433.

6. Ibid.

7. Jules Menken, "Britain and the Persian Question," *The National Review*, vol. 126 (January 1946), p. 26-27.

8. Najafgoli Pesyan, *Marg Bud Bazgast Ham Bud* [There were both death and retreat] (Tehran: 1949), pp. 17-18 (hereafter cited as *Death and Retreat*).

9. Ibid., p. 19.

10. Ibid., p. 20.

11. Ibid., pp. 26-27, 30-32.

12. Hussein Amuzgar, *Naft Va Havades Azerbaijan* [Oil and the events in Azerbaijan] (Tehran: November 1947), pp. 87-90 (hereafter cited as *Oil and Events*).

13. Ibid., pp. 95-97, 99-101.

14. Pesyan, *Death and Retreat*, p. 23.

15. Amidi-Nuri, *Azerbaijan-i Demukrat* [The Azerbaijan democrats] (Tehran, 1946), p. 27.

16. Interview with Dr. Reza Danesh (pseudonym), a former member of the Democratic Party of Azerbaijan, London, 28 August 1971.

17. Amidi-Nuri, Azerbaijan-i Demukrat [The Azerbaijan democrats], p. 28-30.

18. Amuzgar, *Oil and Events*, p. 106.

19. *Mozakerat Majlis* [Majlis debates] (Tehran, 20 October 1945).

20. Amuzgar, *Oil and Events*, pp. 117-18.

21. Pesyan, *Death and Retreat*, p. 29.

22. *New York Times*, 19 November 1945.

23. *Bakhtar*, 19 November 1945; Pesyan, *Death and Retreat*, pp. 30-31.

24. *Bakhtar*, 20 November 1945.

25. *Ettelaat*, 22 November 1945, also Pesyan, *Death and Retreat*, pp. 61-63.

26. Ministry of Foreign Affairs, *Official Journal of Iran*, no. 238, (Tehran: 5 December 1945), p. 825.

27. George Kirk, *The Middle East in the War, Survey of International Affairs, 1939-1946*, 3 vols., (London: Oxford University Press, 1952), 3:59-60.

28. The note was published in *The New York Times*, 9 December 1945.

29. *Mozakerat Majlis* [Majlis debates] (Tehran, 29 November 1945).

30. Amuzgar, *Oil and Events*, pp. 202-12.

31. Ibid., pp. 260-64.

32. Clifton Daniel, "Iran Picks Council to Survey Revolt," *New York Times*, 10 December 1945.

33. Amuzgar, *Oil and Events*, p. 265.

34. Pesyan, *Death and Retreat*, pp. 124-26.

35. Ibid., pp. 127-29.

36. Ibid., pp. 132-34.

37. Ibid., pp. 135-37.

38. Ibid., p. 138; Amidi-Nouri, *Azerbaijan-i Demukrat* [The Azerbaijan Democrats], pp. 29-31.

39. Amuzgar, *Oil and Events*, pp. 389-93.

40. For a complete analysis, see William Eagleton, *The Kurdish Republic of 1946* (London: Oxford University Press, 1963).

41. Amuzgar, *Oil and Events*, pp. 266-68, 386-88.

42. Ibid., pp. 281-88.

43. *Mozakerat Majlis* [Majlis debates] (Tehran, 18 December 1945), pp. 870-73.

44. Ibid., pp. 305-6.

45. James F. Byrnes, *Speaking Frankly* (New York: Harper and Brothers, 1947), p. 118.

46. Ibid., p. 119.

47. Ibid.

48. Ibid., p. 120.

49. *Mozakerat Majlis* [Majlis debates] (Tehran, 7 January 1946), pp. 988-89.

50. Ibid., p. 990.

51. *Bakhtar*, 11 January 1946; Ostovan, *Negative Equilibrium*, 2:223-27.

52. Byrnes, *Speaking Frankly*, p. 123.

53. United Nations, *Official Records of the Security Council* (1st Year, 1st Series, no. 1), pp. 16-17.

54. Ibid., p. 69.

55. "Russian Denial of Iranian Charges," *Current History*, no. 10 (March 1946), pp. 258-60.

56. *Official Records of the Security Council*, no. 1, p. 70.

57. Sephr Zabih, *The Communist Movement in Iran* (Berkeley: University of California Press, 1966), pp. 105-6.

58. Ostovan, *Negative Equilibrium*, 2:245.

4 Premier Qavam, the Soviets, and the Azerbaijan Movement

At age seventy, Ahmad Qavam brought an assuredness and energy to the office of prime minister which were lacking in his predecessors. He had been premier three times before and had opposed Reza Shah's dictatorship. In fact, Qavam had spent that period either in jail or in exile.

After the overthrow of Reza Shah many nationalists, including Dr. Mussadeq, argued that Ahmad Qavam had the ability, experience, and statesmanship necessary both to neutralize the court and the army and to establish an equilibrium in Iran's foreign relations between the Soviets and the British.

As prime minister in 1942, he curbed the power of the army. In his approach to the Russians he had been realistic, trying to convince them that his government was not anti-Soviet. He cooperated with the Allies and engaged American advisors such as Millspaugh and H. Norman Schwarzkopf for finance, gendarmerie, and the office of price stabilization. He was forced to resign because of his disagreements with Mohammed Reza Shah.

In January 1946 the situation in Iran was chaotic, and the entire structure of government was on the verge of collapse. With Azerbaijan having declared its autonomy and the northern provinces under the occupation of the Red army, with a divided Majlis and a demoralized army, with the British doing everything possible to prevent Qavam from becoming premier—the nation again turned to Qavam and he was nominated in the Majlis by a one vote majority. The Soviet embassy let it be known that Qavam was acceptable, and the Tudeh parliamentary faction, for the second time, joined in a vote of confidence for a new government. As in its earlier support for Bayat, the Tudeh faction backed the candidate supported by the Soviets, regardless of his social origins or the nature of the Majlis coalition that voted for him.[1]

Qavam began his official duties by dismissing General Hassan Arfa, the chief of the general staff of the army, who had been assailed by the left-wing press as "Fascist" and a "pro-British reactionary." This was interpreted as a desire on Qavam's part to make his administration more acceptable to the Russians.

In a speech to the Majlis on 18 February Qavam explained that his main task was to create an atmosphere of mutual respect and trust with the Soviet Union. Telling the deputies of a warm message of congratulations from Stalin, he said that in his reply to the Soviet leader he had asked consent to head an Iranian mission to Moscow to negotiate the Irano-Soviet dispute. Stalin had immediately extended an invitation, and Qavam reported that in twenty hours he would be leaving for Moscow.[2]

[Here it should be noted that Hakimi, when he became premier, had sent a similar message to Stalin requesting his approval to visit the Soviet Union—but the Russians never acknowledged Hakimi's request.]

To a desperate nation the invitation to Qavam was interpreted as an encouraging development. The Majlis approved the trip to Moscow with the hope that Qavam would be successful in implementing the withdrawal of Soviet troops from Iran.

Qavam's Mission to Moscow

On 18 February 1946, the Soviets placed a plane at the disposal of Qavam and the eleven other members of the mission to Moscow. Included were three members of the Majlis, the chairman of the chamber of commerce, four journalists, a former ambassador to the Soviet Union (who spoke Russian fluently), an official of the ministry of foreign affairs, and a former cabinet minister.[3]

Qavam was in the Soviet capital from 19 February until 8 March. During this time he met several times with Molotov and twice with Generalissimo Stalin. In the discussions with Molotov, very little was accomplished. Molotov's complaint was that there were elements in Iran who opposed cooperation and friendship with the Russians and that their main objective was to convert Iran into a base against the Soviet Union. He cited Seyyd Zia and his followers as one example.

Qavam answered that the Iranian people had always desired closer ties and good relations with the Soviet Union. He told Molotov that Iran was proud of the success of its northern neighbor and hoped that in the future the Soviets would give aid to Iran's development projects.[4]

Molotov also mentioned negotiating an oil concession in northern Iran, but was informed by Qavam that under the Majlis law he could not negotiate such a concession. "In fact," he added, "I would be subject to a jail sentence under that law."

"Then change the law," Molotov demanded. "Only the Majlis can do that," Qavam demurred.

"Then change the Majlis," Molotov roared. Qavam explained that no new elections could take place as long as there were foreign troops on Iranian soil. "I can help you out with that," Molotov snapped back.[5]

Qavam, discouraged with his discussions with Molotov, met with Stalin on 24 February. The meeting lasted three hours, but the parties failed to reach any agreement.

In their discussion, the Soviets stressed three issues:

1. To prove her friendship, Iran should grant an oil concession in the northern provinces to the Soviet government, especially since the southern oil had been in the hands of the British for many years.
2. Azerbaijan was an internal problem and should be settled between Tehran and Azerbaijan.
3. Complete evacuation of Iran by the Red army would not take place until there was every assurance that Russia would not have a hostile neighbor in the south. Small numbers of Soviet troops would be withdrawn from specific areas starting on 2 March.[6]

A memorandum emphasizing the following points was sent by Qavam to the Soviet government on 26 February:

1. Regarding northern oil—the Majlis had passed a law forbidding any negotiations with a foreign power, therefore, it would not be possible to discuss the issue at that time.
2. Concerning Azerbaijan—this province was an integral part of Iran, and *Farsi* not Turki had always been the official language of the province. There had recently been a revolt against the government of Iran, which was prepared to negotiate and introduce needed reforms, but the proposal for an independent Azerbaijan was not negotiable.
3. Regarding Soviet troops in Iran—the Tripartite Treaty of 1942, ratified by the Majlis, provided that British and Soviet troops should evacuate Iran not later than six months following the end of hostilities, that is, by 2 March 1946. The Soviet Union should trust the friendly intentions of the present government and complete the evacuation of Iran as soon as possible.[7]

The Soviet answer on 28 February outlined the following positions:

1. The Soviet Union was prepared to forego its demand for an oil concession, but called for the establishment of a joint Irano-Soviet stock company for the exploitation of oil in the northern provinces. The Soviet Union would own 51 percent of the shares and Iran 49 percent.

2. Regarding Azerbaijan—it was Iran's internal problem, but the Soviet government recommended that the Iranian government win back the loyalty of the people through the introduction of immediate social, economic, and educational reforms.

   The national Majlis of Azerbaijan should change into a state legislature, and the prime minister of the province should become the governor-general representing the central government.

   Azerbaijan should have neither a minister of war nor a minister of foreign affairs. The commander-in-chief of the army should be appointed by the Iranian government.

3. Concerning the evacuation of Iran by the Red army—Soviet withdrawals from certain areas would start on 2 March. But the complete evacuation depended on Soviet relations with the central government.[8]

Dr. Mussadeq, in a speech to the Majlis, stated that the one-sided foreign policy of previous governments should be held responsible for the present predicament. The results of this diplomacy, according to Mussadeq, had caused Russian mistrust and intransigence, and the failure of past governments to understand this situation had brought Iran to the brink of disaster—needed now were mutual respect and candid negotiations.[9]

The deadline for the withdrawal of Allied troops from Iran was 2 March 1946. The United States forces left Iran by 1

January, and the British evacuated their last troops by that stipulated date. On 1 March, however, Moscow Radio announced that Iranian Premier Qavam had been informed, in Moscow, that the Soviet forces would be withdrawn from certain specific areas—Khorassan, Shahrud and Semnan—but that Soviet forces would remain in other areas until the situation had become clear.[10]

In Moscow, Qavam sent Molotov a letter of protest and reminded the Soviets of the Tripartite Pact concluded in 1942, which established a positive date for the evacuation of all Allied troops.[11]

The military situation deteriorated. The Soviet Union, instead of withdrawing its troops, poured in new forces. Robert Rossow, Jr.* has outlined those troop movements:

> On the night of March 4-5 more tanks began to arrive in Tabriz—46 T-34 mediums came in by rail and were taken to the big tank and artillery park in the center of the barracks area. Troops and armored columns continued marching outward from Tabriz in three directions—toward Turkish and Iraqi frontiers and toward Tehran. On March 6 Marshall Ivan Bagramian, the wartime Commanding General of the Soviet First Baltic Army and a noted authority on armor, arrived in Tabriz and assumed field Command of the new force. . . .Troops glutted the town, the pale blue shoulder marks of the Soviet cavalry being almost entirely replaced by the red-piped black, with gold tank silhouette, of the Soviet armor.[12]

The magnitude of Soviet moves alarmed Washington. Until this time the United States government had followed a passive role in Iran, but now the decision was made by Secretary of State Byrnes and his principal advisers to seize the initiative in the Middle East, a role traditionally left to the British.

Secretary Byrnes comments:

---

* Robert Rossow, Jr. was in charge of the United States Consulate in Tabriz from December, 1945, through June, 1946, and then was Chief of the Political Section of the Embassy in Tehran until January 1947.

At Moscow I still hoped that the Soviet Union and the United States had a common purpose. However, by the latter part of January 1946, there was accumulated evidence that regardless of what might be their long-term plan, certainly their immediate purpose was to delay the peace in Europe and in the Pacific. . . .But even more threatening was the Soviet attitude toward Iran, the evidence of their willingness to violate the sovereignty of their little neighbor. It confirmed the ambition Molotov had expressed to Hitler for the control of the territory south of Baku. These things inspired my speeches beginning in February 1946, speeches which were correctly interpreted as reflecting a firmer attitude toward the Soviet Government. No longer was there any wisdom in minimizing our differences because no longer was there any justification for the belief that we were animated by the common purpose of an early peace.[13]

Following instructions given by Mr. Byrnes, a note was sent to Moscow on 6 March stating that the decision of the Soviet government to retain troops in Iran beyond the period established by the 1942 treaty had caused a situation to which the United States could not remain indifferent.[14]

A second note, couched in far stiffer language, was delivered in Moscow on 9 March. It stated that the United States government had been receiving reports of considerable movements of Soviet combat forces and war materials from the direction of the Soviet frontier toward Tabriz and outward from Tabriz in the direction of Tehran and the Iraqi and Turkish frontiers. The government of the United States desired to learn whether the Soviet government, instead of withdrawing its troops from Iran as urged in the earlier note, was bringing additional forces into the country. If the Soviets were increasing their forces, the American government desired information at once regarding the purposes thereof.

As a pointed warning the Navy department announced on 8 March that the battleship *U.S.S. Missouri* would proceed to Istanbul in two weeks carrying the remains of the Turkish ambassador, who had died at his post in Washington.

The Soviet government did not answer the American note, but *Tass* stated that the reports emanating from Washington "do not correspond with the facts."[15]

Premier Qavam denied that additional Soviet troops had arrived in Iran, but disappointed because of the stalemate with the Soviets he decided to leave Moscow. He asked for a farewell meeting with Stalin. Stalin asked Qavam to postpone his trip for twenty-four hours and invited the Iranian delegation to dine with him.

Stalin complained to Qavam that Iran had taken an unfriendly attitude toward the Soviet Union from the inception of the Communist revolution. He said that he was ready to help Iran but that an immediate change in approach to relations with the Soviet Union would be necessary.

Qavam agreed that past difficulties must be forgotten and assured Stalin that his government's policy would be one of improving and cementing friendly relations between the two nations.

Stalin then told Qavam that Ivan V. Sadchikov would be sent to Tehran as the new Soviet ambassador. Sadchikov would be empowered to eliminate the misunderstandings and negotiate agreements which would strengthen relations between the Soviet Union and Iran.

The general sense of the final communique indicated that from 19 February to 6 March, questions of interest to the two governments had been discussed in an amicable atmosphere. Both governments would exert all efforts so that the appointment of the new Soviet ambassador to Iran would create favorable conditions for consolidation of friendly relations between the two countries.[16]

Nevertheless, the Moscow negotiations had not produced any significant results regarding the three main issues under discussion. The Soviet government was unable to accept Qavam's pressing demand for the withdrawal of troops. The Russians revived their demand for an oil concession to which

Qavam replied, simply, that he was unable to discuss the question in view of the existing Majlis law forbidding oil negotiations with foreign countries. Qavam asked for Soviet moral support in settling the Azerbaijan difficulties but the Russians flatly refused, calling the situation in northern Iran an internal question. The Soviets then asked for the recognition of autonomy for the regime in Azerbaijan, but Qavam explained he could go only so far as provincial council law allowed and could not possibly accept the present arrangement.

With the meetings over and the discussion at an impasse, Qavam returned to Tehran on 10 March. The Fourteenth Majlis was coming to a close, and no new elections could take place as long as foreign troops remained in Iran. The absence of a Majlis would then make Qavam a virtual dictator. A majority of the deputies wished to prolong the mandate of the Fourteenth Majlis in order to avoid leaving the nation without a parliament during a period when crucial decisions had to be made. But for several days Tudeh-organized demonstrations in the Majlis square prevented a quorum from meeting. The Tudeh favored the end of the Majlis and, since Qavam had given support to their aspirations, desired the Premier as the sole ruler.

At the last meeting of the Majlis on 12 March three thousand Tudeh supporters jammed *Baharestan* square and permitted only deputies acceptable to them to pass unmolested. A right-wing deputy who insisted on passage was mauled by the crowd.

Premier Qavam appeared in the Majlis chambers to give an informal report on his trip to Moscow. Only 42 of 112 deputies were present. Since the meeting failed to gather a quorum, no formal vote of confidence was requested or given. With the dissolution of the Fourteenth Majlis, a powerful Ahmad Qavam began the necessary maneuvering which eventually led to the settlement of the Azerbaijan crisis.[17]

Iran's Case before the Security Council

Following the tough policy laid down by Secretary Byrnes, the United States Ambassador in Tehran told Qavam that if his government did not present the Soviet-Iranian differences to the Security Council the United States delegation would do so. To the United States the Iranian case was no longer a local or isolated situation.

Wallace Murray, the American ambassador to Iran, sent a top secret message to Secretary Byrnes on 11 March 1946. In it Murray outlined the result of his discussion with Qavam after his return from Moscow. The following excerpts are quoted from the telegram:

. . .I asked Qavam what he intended to do next. He said he wanted to send full written account to Ala* and asked me to forward it through our pouch. I agreed but pointed out situation was urgent and telegraphic action seemed indicated. He appeared to acquiesce but did not make clear statement as to instructions he would give Ala nor did he say definitely that he would ask further immediate consideration by Security Council. However, he did say that Iran had not and would not withdraw its petition to Security Council. . . .I am seeking another appointment with Prime Minister in a day or two at which time I hope to elicit something more positive. Because Qavam's attitude did not seem entirely clear as regards United Nations Organization action I arranged audience with Shah this morning. I told His Majesty that I had no grounds for suspecting Prime Minister of weakening but would like him (Shah) to make sure Qavam understood situation and vital importance of Iranian action. I am sure Shah is completely clear on this.

His Majesty expressed grave concern over rumors of possible Soviet *Putsch* in Tehran to seize capital and gain control of Government. He pointed out that if this should happen Soviets could dictate instructions to Ala, prevent Iranian appeal to UNO and so make parallel Irano-Ameri-

* Hussein Ala was Iranian ambassador to the United States.

can action impossible. He suggested that in such a case United States and Britain could nevertheless act on own initiative on basis their obligations and voice true Iranian sentiments.

Shah made point that Iranian case is now far more simple and clear cut than at time of London UNO discussion since continued presence of Soviet troops in Iran after March 2 is obvious breach of treaty and makes it unnecessary to demonstrate that Soviet authorities are interfering in any other fashion. I agreed and said that in view of this strengthening of Iranian case it would be utter folly for Iran to weaken at this stage.[18]

In another top secret message sent on 14 March to the secretary of state, Ambassador Murray stated:

> In course of conversation which I consider highly satis-factory I reemphasized utter importance of action by Iran to speak out for herself in defense of her rights so long as she is free to speak. Qavam agreed. . . .I also pointed out that in coming Council meeting Iran could act with ad-vance assurance of U.S. support which it had not had at London meeting.
>
> Since we cannot be sure Iranian Foreign Office will give Ala adequate background information Department may wish to give him substance of such parts of my two recent con-versations with Qavam as it deems appropriate.
>
> Furthermore although I am satisfied with Qavam's assurances it is always possible that Russians will apply great pressure on him when they learn of his decision and try to persuade him to withdraw his instructions. Accord-ingly I suggest Department urge upon Ala importance of immediate action on his part to get matter before Security Council as soon as he receives his instructions. Once case is presented formally it will be easier for Qavam to resist pressure.[19]

Secretary Byrnes later wrote: "It would be necessary for us to oppose the Soviet Government if the case did become a

Security Council issue. . .I outlined in detail the actual course of events in the Security Council and stressed that once Soviet troops had remained in Iran beyond the treaty date, it was no longer possible to arrange matters privately; the issue then had to be met in the light of public opinion."[20]

In an article in *Izvestia*, Nikolai Alexeyev charged that some Iranian statesmen had carried out plans to bring on a collision between the Soviet Union and other great powers. Seyyd Zia was mentioned as one politician who had provoked friction between the Soviet Union and England. Alexeyev emphasized that the role of the Red Army was to defend Soviet territory from such provocations.

Mr. Alexeyev wrote of Russia's friendly actions to help give the Iranian people a free and independent existence, and of Soviet readiness to give aid for the political and economic development of Iran.[21]

The Iranian ambassador to the United States, Hussein Ala, filed a formal notice with the UN secretary general on 18 March, calling attention to the refusal of the Soviet government to remove its troops from Iranian territory and for the placing of Iran's complaint "on the agenda of the Security Council due to meet on March 25th."[22]

On the following day Mr. Andrei Gromyko requested postponement of consideration of the Iranian plea by the Security Council until 10 April, on the grounds that direct negotiations between the two governments were continuing and that the Soviet delegation needed more time for the preparation of its case.

In a note of 20 March to the United Nations Organization the Iranian ambassador requested that action not be delayed, stating that the continued presence of Soviet forces in Iran beyond 2 March was not a proper subject for negotiation under the Charter or the Iranian Constitution. Ala also claimed that delays already encountered had intensified the critical situation in Iran and that further postponements would cause harm to Iranian interests.

President Harry S. Truman, in a press conference held on 21 March 1946, said that the United States government would not agree to postponement of the 25 March meeting and further that it would insist on the immediate consideration of the Iranian case.[23]

In Tehran the government's announcement that it was presenting Iran's case to the Security Council brought a prompt reaction from the Soviet Union and the Tudeh party. The Soviet representative in Tehran told Qavam that his government would regard such an appeal as a hostile act.

On the afternoon of 20 March the new Soviet ambassador, Ivan V. Sadchikov, met with Premier Qavam only a few hours after reaching Tehran, describing himself as surprised and upset on having learned at Baku of the Iranian appeal to the Security Council. He said he thought it had been understood that he was coming to Tehran to continue the Moscow negotiations. Qavam reminded Sadchikov of his protest against continued occupation of Iran filed in Moscow, and said he thought he had made it clear that the presence of Soviet troops in Iran after 2 March tied his hands so far as negotiations were concerned.[24]

In the 21 March issue of *Izvestia*, Nikolai Alexeyev accused some influential members of the Iranian ruling class of promoting hostile activities against the Soviet Union. He also charged that because of the feudal influence of the late Reza Shah Pahlevi's regime, no democratic reforms had been carried out and that the broad masses of the Iranian people were dissatisfied.

Alexeyev listed as needed reforms: free democratic elections to the Majlis; organization of local self government; solution of the nationalities question; liquidation of unemployment; agrarian reform; and the elimination of criminal elements within the government. The article further warned that pro-Fascist elements were trying to involve Iran in political adventures against the Soviet Union and that the continuation of such policies could only lead to further aggravation of the situation in the country.[25]

The Tudeh party organized demonstrations protesting the government's decision to present Iran's case to the Security Council. Russian troops were at Karaj and the Shah, fearful of a Soviet take-over, was getting ready to flee with the court to some other part of the country.

On 23 March, Secretary of State Byrnes sent this top secret message to Ambassador Murray in Tehran:

. . . While we believe it would be better for Shah and Government to remain in Tehran even if this involves some danger or inconvenience, it is recognized that circumstances may develop which make this inadvisable.

If Shah leaves Tehran with his court for purpose of setting up Government at some other place in Iran, you may find it advisable to designate a secretary of Embassy to accompany him. If however he leaves Tehran merely to take refuge elsewhere it seems to us that it would be preferable not to detail a secretary to accompany him. We leave this, however, to your discretion.

The question of the recognition by this Government of a new Government in Iran will of course depend on circumstances. In general we would not recognize a new Government brought about by duress.[26]

Qavam showed himself an astute politician and diplomat. He arrested Seyyd Zia, who for three years had been assailed by the Tudeh party as a pro-British anti-Communist reactionary. He ordered the suspension of all newspapers hostile to the Soviet Union and had his security forces occupy the headquarters of the anti-Tudeh political parties.[27]

In a press conference on 23 March Qavam revealed that, as a result of direct negotiations, it was possible that Soviet troops might begin to withdraw before the meeting of the Security Council two days hence. It therefore did not matter whether the meeting was delayed a week or two. Meanwhile, he instructed Hussein Ala to avoid any statements and actions likely to lead to further misunderstandings, which was taken to be a reprimand for Ala's action in announcing that the Iranian government opposed the Soviet request for a delay in the Security Council meeting. Qavam had been trying to soothe the Russians whenever possible and was upset because Ala had taken action without authorization.

On 24 March the American ambassador (Murray), alarmed at the apparent change in Qavam's position, met with the prime minister and after the meeting sent the following urgent, top secret report to Secretary of State Byrnes:

> I saw Qavam this morning and expressed surprise and concern that he should have made public statements of this kind. I remarked that it seemed curious time for him to appear to belittle importance of Security Council in light of stand taken by United States Government. . .
>
> Qavam replied that correspondents must have misunderstood his remarks which were general in character and that he had not intended to convey impression they seemed to have received. (Since Mozaffar Firuz who is fast becoming Qavam's evil genius acted as interpreter I can believe Prime Minister's remarks may have been distorted in translation.) On my urging he summoned another press conference this morning to correct impression given yesterday. To insure against distortion this time I left my own confidential interpreter Saleh to handle translation.
>
> Qavam said he had not sent any new instructions to Ala regarding presentation of Iranian case to Security Council and that he did not intend to do so unless and until he reached some satisfactory agreement with Soviets here.
>
> In reply to my question Prime Minister said he had not definitely presented to Soviet Ambassador proposal for joint oil exploitation as inducement for withdrawal Soviet troops. However, he still had this idea under active consideration and did not believe Russians would evacuate without this concession. He did not indicate when he planned to broach his suggestion to Sadchikov. . .[28]

On the same day, Soviet Ambassador Sadchikov called on Qavam with three notes, the first of which said that "the Soviet Command in Iran estimates that the complete evacuation of Soviet troops from Iran can be concluded in the course of five to six weeks if nothing unforeseen should take place." The second note proposed that an Irano-Soviet company be formed to develop Iranian oil, fifty-one percent of the profits to be Russian and forty-nine percent Iranian. The third note offered to intercede in the Azerbaijan situation on the basis that the Prime Minister of Azerbaijan should be known as governor general, cabinet ministers should be known as directors of offices, and the local Majlis should be known as the Provincial Council.

Sadchikov called again in the evening to inform Premier Qavam that the Soviet government was pleased to learn of the arrest of Seyyd Zia and announced Soviet intentions to withdraw troops at once from Karaj and Qazvin in accordance with Qavam's request.[29]

Consideration of the Iranian complaint by the Security Council was now skillfully used by Prime Minister Qavam as a lever for extracting better terms from the Soviets.

The Security Council, meeting in New York, took up the question on 26 March. The Soviet ambassador, Mr. Andrei Gromyko, opposed placing the complaint on the agenda, arguing that negotiations between the Soviet government and the government of Iran had resulted in an agreement regarding the evacuation of Soviet troops.[30]

After discussion a Soviet resolution to delete the Iranian item from the agenda was defeated by a vote of nine to two, Poland voting with the Soviet Union. By a similar vote the agenda was adopted, whereupon Mr. Gromyko again proposed that further discussion be postponed until 10 April. Defeated again on this point, on which only the Polish delegate supported him, the Soviet representative and his aides left the Council chamber on 27 March stating that they would not discuss the Iranian issue until 10 April.

Ambassador Hussein Ala was then asked to sit at the delegates' table. Ala said that he knew of no agreement, secret or otherwise, between the two governments on the matter now before the Council. He added that Soviet troops and agents were interfering with internal affairs and that demands had been made on Iran's sovereignty. He stated that a delay would be a threat to peace and then asked for immediate action on the crisis.

On 29 March the Council, with the Soviet delegate absent, and by unanimous vote of ten members, instructed the secretary-general (through a suggestion proposed by American Secretary of State James F. Byrnes) to request that the two governments furnish more information by 3 April on the progress of negotiations, particularly whether or not the reported withdrawal of troops was being made conditional on their reaching an agreement.

The United States ambassador sent a telegram to Secretary Byrnes on 3 April informing him that "in press conference today Prince Firouz* revealed Ala would inform Security Council that Soviet note of March 25 regarding withdrawal of Soviet troops did not contain any qualifications."[32]

The Security Council met on the same day to consider the replies from the governments of the Soviet Union and Iran. The Soviet reply to the Council's request for information stated that negotiations had led to an understanding regarding the withdrawal of the Russian troops from Iran and that other questions were not connected with the withdrawal.

The Iranian reply stated that negotiations had not achieved "positive results" and that Soviet agents, officials, and armed forces continued to interfere in Iranian internal affairs. It was pointed out that on 24 March the Soviet ambassador to Iran had informed the Iranian prime minister that evacuation of

---

* Prince Mozaffar Firouz was Deputy Prime Minister and Director of Propaganda under Qavam. He later became Minister of Labor and Propaganda. He was a key figure in the negotiations with the Soviet Union and Pishevari.

Soviet troops from Iran within a period of five or six weeks was on the condition that no unforeseen circumstances should occur. Three days later, in another conversation with Qavam, the same Soviet representative said that there would be no further cause for anxiety and that no "unforeseen circumstances" would take place if agreement could be reached on the question of oil concessions and an autonomous government for Azerbaijan.

After the replies were read, Secretary of State Byrnes asked Ala whether in the light of the communiques he had any suggestions to make regarding Security Council action.

Ala answered that his government would be willing not to press for the consideration of the matter at this time, provided the Soviet Union was willing to remove the condition of "unforeseen circumstances" relating to the withdrawal of troops and give the Security Council assurance that the troops would be evacuated unconditionally not later than 6 May, and provided that these matters remain on the Council's agenda for consideration at any time.[33]

Accordingly, on 4 April, the Council, by vote of nine to zero with Australia abstaining, adopted a resolution introduced by Secretary Byrnes deferring further proceedings on the Iranian appeal until 6 May, at which time both parties were requested to report whether all Soviet troops had been withdrawn from the whole of Iran. The Soviet delegate still did not attend the session.[34]

Documents reveal that Premier Qavam was furious at Ala's performance and especially disturbed by Ala's comments in the Security Council, as the ambassador had gone beyond his instructions. Qavam said he had never told Ala to assert the Soviet intention to evacuate without condition if satisfactory agreements were reached on other points.

It was after learning of Ala's declaration that Qavam sent for Sadchikov and proposed to him the issuance of a communique. Sadchikov was highly annoyed by Ala's remarks, since on the previous day he and the premier had agreed that both the Iranian and the Soviet representatives would formally assure the Security Council that troop withdrawals were unconditional. The Soviet ambassador complained that Qavam said one thing in Tehran and another thing through his representative in New York. The prime minister told Sadchikov that was water over the dam and persuaded him to agree to a communique in order to remedy matters.[35]

Questioned on the role of Hussein Ala at the United Nations, Mr. Mozaffar Firouz declared:

> The task was extremely delicate and difficult. The whole question was being debated in the United Nations and Ala was our representative. I persuaded Qavam after long discussions with the Soviet representatives that the only way to settle the international aspect of the Azerbaijan question and secure the withdrawal of Soviet troops was in direct negotiations with the Soviet government. That, discussion in the United Nations forum would only make things worse as Ala, instead of carrying out our instructions, was on the order of others. He was every day making provocative statements against the Soviet government, which made them suspicious of our good faith and real motives. In spite of several harsh telegrams to Ala, which would have resulted in any honorable person resigning his post, he continued his provocations.[36]

A joint communique was issued by Qavam and Sadchikov on 4 April, announcing that an agreement had been reached. In the accord, the Soviets pledged to evacuate Iran within one and one-half months after 26 March 1946. Iran agreed, tentatively, to an oil concession in the form of a joint Irano-Soviet company to be established in the north. With regard to Azerbaijan, a pledge was made that the problem would be resolved peacefully in accordance with existing laws and "in a benevolent spirit toward the people of Azerbaijan."[37]

At a press conference on the same day the government spokesman Mozaffar Firouz stated that Majlis law prohibited only the granting of oil while the country was occupied and did not prevent the formation of an oil company financed by Iranian and Soviet capital. He added that before such a company could be formed it must be approved by the Majlis, but that elections for the fifteenth Majlis could not be held until all the Russian troops were out of the country. Prince Firouz also said that "as a result of these negotiations. . .all outstanding questions have been settled on a basis of complete reciprocity and good will." He said the agreement had received the unanimous approval of the Cabinet.[38] The announcement showed that contrary to previous declarations, the withdrawal of the Soviet troops had not been unconditional but was connected with the questions of oil and Azerbaijan.

Details of the agreement elaborating upon the major terms of the oil understanding were published in Tehran on 8 April:

1. The Iranian and Soviet governments had agreed to establish a joint Irano-Soviet company to explore and exploit oil producing territories in northern Iran.

2. The company was to operate for a period of fifty years.

3. During the first twenty-five years of the company's operations, 49 percent of the shares would be held by Iran and 51 percent by the Soviet Union. During the second twenty-five years, both governments would control the shares on an equal basis.

4. Profits accruing to the company would be divided in proportion to the shares of each party.

5. Territory to be covered by the company's operations were Gilan, Mazanderan, Gorgan, Northern Khorassan, and part of Azerbaijan east of the line drawn southeast from the junction of Irano-Soviet-Turkish frontiers along the eastern side of Lake Rezaieh and reaching the city of Miandoab. Meanwhile, the Iranian government would not grant a concession in the territory situated west of the said line to foreign

companies or to Iranian companies with foreign participation or employing foreign capital.

6. On the Iranian side the capital was to consist of the oil bearing lands, mentioned above, which after technical operations would contain oil wells, the produce of which might be useful for the company. On the Soviet side the capital was to include any kind of expenditures involved, instruments, equipment, and the salaries of the experts and laborers who would be needed for the extraction and refining of oil.

7. After the expiration of the period of the company's operation the Iranian government would have the right to purchase the shares belonging to the Soviet Union or to prolong the period of the operation of the company.

8. The protection of the lands subject to exploration, the oil wells and all installations of the company would be carried out exclusively by the security forces of Iran.

9. The accord for the establishment of the company was to be presented for ratification by the new Majlis, as soon as it had been elected and had begun its legislative activity—in any case, not later than seven months after 24 March of the current year.

As stipulated, the Qavam-Sadchikov agreement met the minimum goals of both nations: for Iran, the evacuation of Soviet troops from the north; for the Soviets, an oil concession and the pledge of compromise with the Democratic party of Azerbaijan. Closer analysis revealed a major victory for Qavam-Firouz diplomacy—the compact on the oil company could not become law until ratified by the Fifteenth Majlis, and general elections for that body could be held only after the normalization of the situation throughout the country, including the settlement of the Azerbaijan dispute.

Another important consideration of this agreement was that while the independent government of Tabriz existed, the Soviet government recognized the sovereign rights of Tehran over Azerbaijan. It would now be in the interests of the Soviets to move for a quick settlement between Tehran and the Azerbaijan rebels.

Mozaffar Firouz, discussing the delicate negotiations with the Soviet Union, later said:

> In view of the situation, I summoned the Soviet Ambassador and told him that we desired to have good neighborly relations with the Soviet Union but we could not continue our policy unless the Soviet government showed also its good faith; first, by the immediate withdrawal of its troops from Iran and second, by putting an end to its intolerable support of the Azerbaijan Communist movement. I told Sadchikov that unless we received immediate satisfaction, we would proclaim to the Iranian people and world opinion that the Soviet Union was acting hand in glove with British imperialism, with the view to the *de facto* division of Iran on the 1907 basis. I turned his attention to the fact that we would arm the people and then resign—that the country would fall in a state of anarchy and Soviet troops would be confronted with the armed resistance of the Iranian people. The world would well understand that a new imperialism was being practiced by Lenin's successors. The Soviet Ambassador asked me for several days in order to consult his government. Within a few days the answer arrived, and an official Irano-Soviet communique was circulated announcing the complete withdrawal of all Soviet troops from Iran within a month and one-half, an oil accord and a pledge for a peaceful settlement of the Azerbaijan dispute.
>
> Few people understand what a great success this act constituted for Iranian independence and integrity. As you know Soviet troops remained in Austria for over ten years before an arrangement was made for their withdrawal. With Soviet diplomacy showing a favorable trend, we decided to press our advantage and insist on a settlement of the Azerbaijan question.

Ambassador Murray's analysis of this situation for Secretary Byrnes is also worth relating:

Qavam feels, perhaps correctly, that some part of oil concession to Russia must and should be made eventually. If this is true it might as well come now, when it can help resolve extremely delicate international situation.

While Soviet oil concession, northern Iran, presents obvious danger of Soviet penetration in this country it does not, of course, represent any actual or potential loss to United States in oil, since there is no possibility that we could get concession in that area. Even if we could, it is my understanding its exploitation by us would be commercially impracticable because of great transportation costs to Persian Gulf involved. . .With international relations so strained in all parts of the world, I would hesitate to reject any solution of Iranian problem which would be reasonably satisfactory and would permit our Government and UNO to turn to the many other pressing problems confronting them.

In summary, much as I regret possibility that Iran will be forced to pay bribe to secure what would be accorded her automatically as of right, I do not feel that proposed solution is too bad. . .If plan goes through it should provide reasonable basis for improved Irano-Soviet relations despite fact that it leaves many openings for possible future difficulties. We cannot, after all, provide Iran with an insurance policy against all potential dangers.

Furthermore, I would consider that contemplated agreement would be at least partial victory for U. S. Government and UNO, since I am absolutely certain Russians would have forced their demands to limit if it had not been for firm stand taken by America in upholding UNO Charter. Iranians realize that if Russian troops leave Iran it will be solely due to our action, and they are immensely grateful.[41]

At the Security Council, the Soviets did not relish being called before the court of "world public opinion." This contention was borne out by Ambassador Gromyko's letter of 7 April to the Council in which he stated:

On 26 March, when the Security Council proceeded to consider the Iranian Government's statement of 18 March regarding the delay in the withdrawal of Soviet troops from Iran, I proposed, under instructions from the Soviet Government, that this question should not be considered by the Security Council. . .

The Security Council, however, did not agree with the Soviet Government and retained the question on the agenda. In the meantime. . .on 4 April an understanding on all points was reached between the Soviet and the Iranian Governments. . . .The Soviet Government, moreover, cannot ignore the resolution adopted by the Security Council on 4 April. Under this resolution the Security Council decided to continue the consideration of the Iranian question 6 May despite the fact that on 3 April the Soviet Government stated that the question of the evacuation of Soviet troops had been settled by an understanding reached between the Soviet and the Iranian Governments. . .Under the Charter, the Security Council may investigate any dispute or any situation which might endanger the maintenance of international peace and security. It is, however, quite obvious that, in fact, such a position did not and does not exist in Iran, so that the Security Council had no reason to give further consideration to the Iranian question on 6 May. Accordingly, the above-mentioned resolution of the Security Council of 4 April is incorrect and illegal, being in conflict with the Charter of the United Nations.

For the above-mentioned reasons the Soviet Government insists that the Iranian question should be removed from the agenda of the Security Council.[42]

Qavam was pressured by Soviet Ambassador Sadchikov to withdraw the Iranian complaint from the Security Council. He said that Iran's insistence on the continuance of the case was an insult to the Soviet Union that would not be tolerated.

The representative of the United States also pressed Qavam to depend on the United Nations for security. The premier was told that any move on his part to have the Iranian case dropped from the agenda of the Security Council would create an impression on world opinion and among members of the Council that Iran wished to have the United Nations act merely to help it in its negotiations and not because it believed, as it stated, that the presence of troops of another government threatened international peace. Iran's most urgent appeal was that this case remain on the agenda until foreign troops had withdrawn. The Council had granted that request. If the government of Iran now wished to have the case removed from the agenda before the troops were withdrawn, how could it thereafter expect any government to give serious attention to its appeals?

The advice given to Qavam, in the interest of Iran and of developing a United Nations strong enough to maintain peace, was that he take the attitude that keeping the question on the agenda was a matter for the Security Council alone to decide.[43]

On 15 April, at the meeting of the Security Council, Mr. Gromyko sharply challenged the action taken in his absence in retaining the Iranian appeal on the agenda. Ambassador Gromyko argued that the vote of 4 April was contrary both to the spirit and the letter of the Charter (Article 34), since the situation did not constitute a threat to peace and security of the world. He then introduced a motion to delete the Iranian request from the agenda.[44]

On the same date the Council received a statement from Iran voicing complete confidence in the word and pledge of the Soviet Union and, therefore, withdrawing its complaint from the Security Council.

The action of Iran in withdrawing its appeal presented a new problem in procedure. At the 16 April meeting of the Council Mr. Stettinius, the United States representative, stated that it was within the power of the Council to continue the Iranian question on the agenda, even though Iran had withdrawn its complaint. He pointed out that the basic factor in the case was the presence of Soviet troops in Iran and that the present circumstances did not justify a reversal of Council's resolution of 4 April.

At the same time, the Council was in receipt of a

memorandum from Secretary-General Trygve Lie in which he affirmed that, since action by the Council had been initiated under Article 35, Paragraph 1, Iran's request to withdraw the appeal removed the basis for continued consideration of the dispute unless the Council desired to vote to investigate under Article 34. This letter was referred to the Committee of Experts for study.

In the ensuing discussion it was pointed out that the Council must have wide latitude in the determination of its procedure with respect to any particular case before it.

The representative of the Netherlands, Mr. Van Kleffens, believed the question at issue was: "Who is master of the Council's agenda, the Council, or States who are parties to a dispute or situation?" He felt that only the Security Council could determine what was and what was not on the agenda.

The French delegate, Mr. Bonnet, proposed a compromise motion which noted that the government of Iran had withdrawn its complaint from the Security Council, called attention to the agreement reached between the governments of the Soviet Union and Iran, and instructed the secretary-general to collect the necessary information to complete the Security Council's report for submission to the General Assembly in September. Action on the motion was deferred until receipt of the report of the Committee of Experts.[45]

At the thirty-sixth meeting of the Council on 23 April, the Committee of Experts reported, in a majority opinion, that the Security Council alone should decide of which matters it is "seized."

The Soviet delegate said the fact that the report was not a unanimous agreement led to the conclusion that the experts followed the instructions of the heads of their delegations. Mr. Gromyko pointed out that the secretary-general's memorandum on the legal aspects of the Iranian case had concluded that the Council could not deny a sovereign state the right to withdraw an appeal.

The American representative stated that he was unable to

agree with the conclusions reached by the secretary-general. Mr. Stettinius agreed that the secretary-general's memorandum disclosed a rather limited concept of the functions of the Security Council that, if accepted, would have serious consequences for the future of that body. He emphasized that the United States strongly supported the opinion offered by the majority of the Committee of Experts.

The representative of France made a strong appeal for his resolution, which he had offered at a previous meeting, calling on the secretary-general to compile a report on the Iranian question for submission to the General Assembly in September.

The Council agreed that the French resolution could be considered as an amendment to the Soviet request to strike the Iranian question from the agenda. After Mr. Gromyko associated himself with the proposal, the Council defeated the motion with only three affirmative votes (USSR, Poland, and France).

Mr. Gromyko inquired about his proposal and was informed by the chairman that there were three votes in favor and eight in opposition. He then declared that since his government considered the retention of the Iranian question on the agenda as contrary to the Charter, he would be unable to take part in any future discussions in the Council on that question.[46]

Ala informed the Council on 6 May that official investigation by his government had shown that Soviet troops had been completely evacuated from the provinces of Khorassan, Gorgan, Mazanderan, and Gilan. "Through other sources," the report said the government had been informed that the evacuation of Azerbaijan would be completed before 7 May; but, because of the interferences previously complained of, the Iranian government officials had exercised no effective authority in the province since 7 November 1945 and had, therefore, been unable to verify these reports by direct observation. "As soon as the Iranian government is able to ascertain through its official representative the true state of affairs in the Province of Azerbaijan, the facts will be reported promptly to the Council."[47]

The Council again considered the matter on 8 May 1946 with the Soviet Union not represented. On motion of Mr. Stettinius, the time for a final report was advanced to 20 May by the unanimous vote of the ten members present.

The Security Council took up the Iranian dispute on 22 May. The Council had before it two Iranian statements: One of 20 May from Ambassador Ala, which stated that no independent investigation of Azerbaijan had been possible and concluded that conditions set by the Security Council had not been fulfilled; the second of 21 May, from the Iranian government, which pointed out that the prime minister had sent a commission to Azerbaijan to investigate regions such as Tabriz and its suburbs. The prime minister's message added that reports from the scene were to the effect that no trace whatever of Soviet troops, equipment, or means of transport were found and that according to "trustworthy people," who were questioned in the area, Soviet troops evacuated Iran on 6 May. Because of the uncertainty as to just what the two statements meant, Hussein Ala was asked to take seat at the Council table.

In answer to a series of questions from the Polish representative, Ala said that the government of Iran was not in authority in Azerbaijan; that he knew of no interference from any other large power; and that his government was faced with a hostile army in Azerbaijan, which was created under Soviet supervision and which would not let the regular Iranian army into that area.

Ala claimed that there were in fact two aspects to the Iranian matter: the presence of the Soviet troops in Iran after 2 March, and the charges that, quite apart from the question of troops, the Soviet Union had been interfering in the internal affairs of Iran. Ala felt the official statement transmitted on 21 May covered the first question but not the second.

No general conclusions were reached on Ala's claim, and on the motion by the Dutch representative, Van Kleffens, it was voted nine to one, that the Security Council "adjourn the discussion of the Iranian question until a date in the near future, the Council to be called together at the request of any member."[48]

This was the last step taken by the Security Council on the Iranian question. On 23 May, a Tass radio broadcast from Moscow emphasized the fact that the evacuation of Soviet troops from Iran had been completed on 9 May.

Ala's attitude and remarks at the Council meeting caused serious embarrassment and difficulties for Premier Qavam. Ambassador Sadchikov accused him of double dealing and hypocrisy, since Premier Qavam had assured the Soviet ambassador that he was satisfied all Soviet troops had left Iran and would report definitively to the Council to this effect. Qavam was contemplating the recall of Ala and sent him a telegram, instructing him to categorically withdraw from the Security Council any statements Ala had made beyond his instructions.

The United States Department of State moved to save Ala's position. Secretary Byrnes sent an urgent message to the new American ambassador to Iran, George V. Allen,* "to use your influence so that Qavam will not recall or repudiate Ala." Byrnes further stated: "We feel that recall or repudiation of Ala at this time would impair ability of Council to give aid to Iran and hope Qavam will refrain from taking precipitous action against Ala under Soviet pressure. Ala has told us that, while he may have gone beyond specific instructions in certain instances, he feels he has properly interpreted Qavam's factual cables and has taken action which Qavam would instruct, if Iran were not under Soviet pressure. . . .It should be stated, Ala has followed his course of action on own decision and has not been influenced by Department to go beyond his instructions."[49]

A compromise was worked out between Qavam and Ambassador Allen in which Ala was instructed to return to Washington, but without withdrawing his credentials as the representative of Iran to the United Nations. On 29 May, the Iranian Embassy in Washington stated that Premier Qavam had instructed Hussein Ala not to make any further statements to the Security Council about the Soviet-Iranian dispute.[50]

One final point: The transcript of President Truman's press and radio conference of 24 April 1952, shows that in 1945 he had sent an ultimatum to the head of the Soviet Union to get out of Persia. The president said that "they got out because we were in a position to meet a situation of that kind."

Later the same day, a White House spokesman made a remark to the press that "the President was using the term ultimatum in a non-technical layman sense." He said that the president was referring to United States leadership in the United Nations, particularly in the Security Council and through diplomatic channels, in the spring of 1946 "which was the major factor in bringing about Soviet withdrawal from Iran."[51]

In *Truman Speaks*, President Truman also makes the following observation: "When Stalin refused to move out of Iran at the time agreed, I sent him word I would move the fleet as far as the Persian Gulf. He got out."[52]

Yet documents published by the Department of State reveal the following: "No documentation on the sending of an ultimatum to the Soviet Union has been found in the Department files or in the files of the Department of Defense, nor have several of the highest officers of the Department in 1946 been able to affirm the sending of an ultimatum."[53]

The Iranian question in the United Nations has become a classical example of the success of the United Nations and the assistance that organization can give to the achievement of the aspirations of smaller states. Although it is exceptionally difficult to evaluate the role of the United Nations in this question, it is worth attempting to weigh the influence it exerted.

First of all, it must be borne in mind that the United Nations settled but little about Iran's charge that the Soviet Union had been interfering in the domestic affairs of the country. Although this was the substance of Iran's complaint presented to the Security Council, that body did not reach any decision or deliberate at length on the charges of interference; nor did the Iranian delegation press for any decision. The entire question was constructed around the withdrawal of Soviet troops from Iran, and the Iranian nation did witness the complete withdrawal of those forces. Moreover, it should be borne in mind that, while in 1946 peoples and nations had a somewhat idealistic image and an unrealistic expectation of the United Nations, the Iranian government was shrewd enough to take account of that organization's limitations. Many authors have expressed the belief that, by appealing to the United Nations, a small nation such as Iran could put all its hope and trust in this international organization to render justice and force a giant power to withdraw its troops.

This was not the case of Iran; on the contrary, the Iranian government used the United Nations as a moral lever and did not consider it a formidable weapon. The insistence of the Iranian delegation that it regretted to bring "this unfortunate situation" to the attention of the Security Council and that it did not consider the "bringing of a dispute before the Security Council" a hostile action indicates that the Iranian government did not desire to put all its hopes in the United Nations at the cost of alienating the Soviet Union. Fortunately, the government of Iran was astute enough to realize that, with twelve hundred miles of common border with Russia, with the presence of Soviet troops in Iran, and with the limitation of the power of the United Nations, it would be much wiser to show a conciliatory attitude while adhering to its goal of preserving Iranian territorial independence. Had Iran tried to act along the same lines as had Ethiopia in the previous decade the outcome would have been far different. The United Nations, unable to take credit for solving the Iranian question, would have failed to receive badly needed prestige; likewise, Iran would have failed to secure its objective of preserving its sovereignty.

Notes

1. Hussein Amuzgar, *Naft Va Havades Azerbaijan* [Oil and the Events in Azerbaijan] (Tehran: November 1947), p. 227 (hereafter cited as *Oil and Events*).

2. Ibid., p. 375.

3. Quassem Massudi, *Jarayan Mossaferat Mission Azemie Iran be Moscow* [An account of the Iranian mission to Moscow] (Tehran: Printing Association Inc., 1947), p. 4 (hereafter cited as *Mission to Moscow*).

4. Ibid., pp. 59-62.

5. "Russia: Inside Story of the Squeeze on Iran," *Newsweek*, 25 March 1946, p. 42.

6. Massudi, *Mission to Moscow*, p. 66.

7. Ibid., pp. 67-68.

8. Ibid., pp. 69-70.

9. *Mozakerat Majlis* [Majlis debates] (Tehran, 29 February 1946), pp. 1097-98.

10. *Dad*, 1 March 1946; *New York Times*, 2 March 1946.

11. *Dad*, 3 March 1946; *New York Times*, 4 March 1946.

12. Robert Rossow, Jr., "The Battle of Azerbaijan, 1946," *Middle East Journal* (winter 1956), p. 20.

13. James F. Byrnes, *Speaking Frankly* (New York: Harper and Brothers, 1947), p. 225.

14. United States, *Department of State Bulletin* (17 March 1946), p. 435.

15. Rossow, "The Battle of Azerbaijan", pp. 22-23.

16. Massudi, *Mission to Moscow*, pp. 149-50, 156-57, 196, 200.

17. Hussein Kay Ostovan, *Slasat-i-Movazereh-i-Manfiey Dar Majlis Chardahom* [Establishment of a Negative Equilibrium in the Fourteenth Majlis] vol. 2. (Tehran: Tabin Press, 1951) 2:246-47 (hereafter cited as *Negative Equilibrium*); *New York Times*, 12 March 1946.

18. Department of State, *Foreign Relations of the United States, the Near East and Africa, 1946*, vol. 7, (Washington: Government Printing Office, 1969), pp. 353-54 (hereafter cited as *Foreign Relations of the United States*).

19. Ibid., p. 355.

20. Byrnes, *Speaking Frankly*, p. 126.

21. *Bakhtar*, 13 March 1946; *New York Times*, 14 March 1946.

22. *Foreign Relations of the United States*, p. 365.

23. Ibid., p. 372.

24. Ibid., pp. 369-70.

25. *New York Times*, 22 March 1946.

26. *Foreign Relations of the United States*, p. 376.

27. Amidi-Nuri, Azerbaijan-i Demukrat [the Azerbaijan Democrats] (Tehran, 1946), p. 31.

28. Ibid., p. 377.

29. Ibid., pp. 379-80.

30. United States, *Department of State Bulletin* (7 April 1946), p. 568.

31. United Nations, *Official Records of the Security Council* (1st Year, 1st Series, no. 2), pp. 35-82.

32. *Foreign Relations of the United States*, p. 402.

33. *Official Records of the Security Council*, no. 2, pp. 83, 87.

34. Ibid., pp. 88-89, 97.

35. *Foreign Relations of the United States*, pp. 406-7.

36. Presentation of Prince Mozaffar Firouz, Paris, 30 May 1969.

37. Najafgoli Pesyan, *Marg Bud Bazgast Ham Bud* [there were both death and retreat] (Tehran: 1949) pp. 203-4 (hereafter cited as *Death and Retreat*); *New York Times*, 6 April 1946.

38.. Ibid.

39. Iranian text in Ostovan, *Negative Equilibrium*, 2:247-48; English text in *Foreign Relations of the United States*, pp. 413-14.

40. Firouz (Presentation), Paris, 30 May 1969.

41. *Foreign Relations of the United States*, pp. 374-75.

42. Ibid., pp. 410-11.

43. Ibid., pp. 419-20.

44. *Official Records of the Security Council*, no. 2, pp. 123-25.

45. For the full text of the proceedings of the Security Council on 16 April, see Ibid., pp. 142-52.

46. Ibid., pp. 200-14.

47. *Foreign Relations of the United States*, p. 451.

48. For the record of the proceedings of the Security Council on 22 May, see *Official Records of the Security Council*, no. 2, pp. 287-305.

49. *Foreign Relations of the United States*, pp. 477-81.

50. Ibid., p. 481, 487.

51. Ibid., p. 348.

52. Harry S. Truman, *Truman Speaks* (New York: Columbia University Press, 1960), p. 71.

53. *Foreign Relations of the United States*, p. 349.

5 The Collapse of the Azerbaijan Insurgency

The Qavam-Sadchikov agreement prompted action by the Soviet Union for the settlement of the Azerbaijan dispute. The Soviets reasoned that a reconciliation between the central government of Iran and Pishevari would allow Azerbaijan to elect a substantial number of deputies to the Fifteenth Majlis who, with the help of other pro-Soviet deputies, would ensure ratification of the oil accord. Premier Qavam also moved to cultivate Soviet confidence and good will by forcibly eliminating the most outspoken anti-Soviet politicians and journalists from the scene.

The Tudeh was calling for the arrest of General Hassan Arfa, who was accused of treason against the people, subservience to Western imperialism, mass killing of the progressive elements, and of supporting "the reactionary palace clique."[1] Hassan Arfa was arrested on 9 April 1946. Mozaffar Firouz declared that Arfa had been arrested for treason, sedition, and association with brigands, and that he would be tried in due time.[2]

Recalling the arrest, Arfa writes: "I was informed that I had been arrested by order of the Prime Minister, in accordance with Article 5 of Martial Law, which provided that persons suspected of activity against the government could be arrested without a regular warrant being issued and

kept under arrest without trial for as long as the Military
Governor should consider it necessary."[3]

The United States charge d'affaires in Iran sent the following secret telegram to the secretary of state on 25 April 1946 to
describe the political situation in Tehran:

. . .Qavam is evidently attempting to appease Russians
wherever possible but at same time endeavoring to stop
short of position in which his Government would become
outright puppet. In pursuing this policy he has: (a) made
oil deal, (b) offered quite liberal terms to Azerbaijan, (c)
vacillated in his position with reference to Security Council
and ultimately yielded to Soviet pressure in asking that case
be dropped, (d) arrested Seyid Zia-ed-Din, General Arfa,
and certain lesser lights hostile to Russians; suppressed
most outspoken anti-Soviet newspapers, and released from
suspension all Left publications; transferred or dismissed
many army officers and government officials considered
anti-Soviet, (e) removed ban on Tudeh meetings; appointed
or permitted appointment of many Tudeh members or
sympathizers to posts in government; definitely recognized
Tudeh labor organization (although labor unions have no
legal status in Iran) and even appointed its leader, Rusta,
as member of new High Labor Council, (f) consistently
been conciliatory in his public statements regarding Azerbaijan question and issued positive orders to security forces
to refrain from attacking or provoking Democrats and not
to enter Azerbaijan until given specific permission by himself.

On the other side of picture, Qavam successfully rejected
most extreme Russian demands on Azerbaijan and oil, did
appeal to Security Council and follow through up to certain
point in face of strong Soviet pressure, and has backed up
Schwarzkopf* in carrying out program of gendarmerie rein-
forcement in Caspian provinces as Russians evacuated.
Prime Minister has ordered all members of all parties in
Caspian area to turn in arms by May 12 and has ordered
gendarmerie to maintain order regardless of who may attempt disturb security. . .

---

* Col. H. Norman Schwarzkopf, Chief of the American Military Mission with the
Iranian gendarmerie. Raised to rank of Brigadier General in July 1946.

Embassy is still of opinion Qavam is acting as sincere patriot and has not sold out to Russians in any way.[4]

A significant point to remember is that Qavam wanted to convince Moscow he desired friendly relations, without making concessions that would compromise Iran's territorial sovereignty. Thus Qavam's internal policy was closely tied to his foreign policy, and consisted mainly in removing grounds for foreign assertions that Iran was so weak she could not manage her affairs or maintain effective internal control. To accomplish this the prime minister moved to reform the security forces and to reorganize domestic institutions.

Qavam encouraged and assisted Schwarzkopf in making the gendarmerie more efficient. He created a Higher Labor Council, composed of representatives of government, the Tudeh labor organization, business, university professors, and the mayor of Tehran. Its objective was to establish programs leading to: better employer-worker relations; draft a new labor law; plan reforms in landlord-tenant relationships on farms; and study ways to affect government economies. He ordered the Ministry of Agriculture to plan agricultural improvements, including new schools and irrigation projects, and established a Supreme Economic Council to develop a five-year economic plan.[5]

Negotiations with Azerbaijan Democrats

With the Russians pressuring Qavam to move on the elections for the Fifteenth Majlis, the prime minister decided to press his advantage and insist on a settlement of the Azerbaijan question while Soviet diplomacy still favored him.

Events in Tehran were moving rapidly. On 22 April Tehran radio broadcast the Iranian government's proposals for Azerbaijan:

1. Agriculture, trade, industry, communication, education, health, police, justice, and finance officers

would be selected by the provincial council and confirmed by the central government.

2. A governor-general would be appointed by the central
government in agreement with the provincial council.

3. The commander of the army and the commandant of
the gendarmerie would be appointed by the central
government.

4. The official language of the province would remain
Farsi, but official work could continue in *Azari-
Turkic*.

5. The activities of democratic political organizations
and workers' unions in Azerbaijan would be free.

6. No action would be taken against the people of Azerbaijan respecting any part taken by them in the
Democratic Party.

7. A bill would be submitted to the next Majlis to increase the number of deputies from Azerbaijan to
correspond with the real population of that province.[6]

An Azerbaijan mission led by Pishevari arrived in Tehran
on 28 April. The negotiations were protracted but brought no
results, as Pishevari insisted on three points which were not
acceptable to the central government. His demands were (a)
the right of the Azerbaijan government to appoint the com-
manders of the Azerbaijan army and gendarmerie; (b) the
right of the Azerbaijan government to appoint the governor of
the province and (c) the distribution of state-owned land to the
peasants.[7]

Pishevari left for Tabriz on 10 May. Premier Qavam thereupon issued a communique calling the Azerbaijan proposals
both unconstitutional and contrary to existing statutes. He
reminded the Azerbaijanis of the constitutional restraints on
his power and emphasized that only after a settlement could
elections for the Fifteenth Majlis be held.[8]

The premier was now asserting his leadership, since he had

gained the upper hand when the Red Army evacuated Iran on 9 May 1946 during Pishevari's stay. Commenting on the breakdown of the negotiations, Mozaffar Firouz later said:

> During these talks which I conducted with the Tabriz representatives, I soon found out that not one amongst them had even the elementary conception of leadership, nothing to say of statesmanship. Instead of thinking of helping to build a new democratic Iran from the Aras to the Persian Gulf, they talked about the narrow limits of Azerbaijan, of having their own government and of talking the Turkish language and eliminating Iranian culture and language, etc. I proposed that they participate with the government in the construction of a new Iran, but they were blinded by their own small and narrow-minded conceptions, and, our discussion being negative, they returned to Tabriz.[9]

However, the break in negotiations with the Azerbaijan leaders was not final. Both the Soviets and the Iranian government had good reasons for wanting them to continue. The Soviets had a vested interest in a quick normalization of the Azerbaijan dispute, for the main proviso of the Qavam-Sadchikov agreement had subjected the granting of the oil concession to approval by the Fifteenth Majlis. It had further imposed a seven-month deadline for submitting the draft agreement to the new Majlis. General elections across the nation would include the rebellious Azerbaijan province, and Qavam had shrewdly established the position that there could be no elections until all of Iran was under the control of the central government. For the Iranian government, it was imperative to pursue policies aimed at neutralizing foreign intervention and asserting the independence and territorial integrity of Iran without bloodshed.

On 11 June Prince Mozaffar Firouz, Qavam's deputy and Director of Propaganda, led an official mission to Tabriz to reopen the talks with Pishevari and to work out the details for accepting the province back under the jurisdiction of the government. Received by a guard of honor and led through cheering crowds, he needed only two days to sign a fifteen-point agreement which was within the framework of the Iranian constitution. Some of the major provisions were:

1. The Azerbaijan Majlis was recognized as the provincial council.
2. The central government would appoint the governor-general, chosen from a panel nominated by the provincial council.
3. The central government agreed to incorporate the Azerbaijan army into the Iranian army, with a joint commission arranging the details.
4. Azerbaijan's irregular soldiers were to become part of the national gendarmerie, with a joint commission arranging the details.
5. The Azerbaijan treasury was to receive 75 percent of the taxes collected in the province, with the central government receiving the rest.
6. The central government agreed to finish the construction of the Azerbaijan railway lines from Mianeh to Tabriz.
7. The central government agreed to assist in the establishment of an Azerbaijan university.
8. *Farsi* and *Azari-Turkic* were recognized as official languages. *Azari-Turkic* was to be taught on the primary level and along with *Farsi* in the secondary and higher schools.
9. Azerbaijan was to receive increased representation in the Iranian Majlis, and a new electoral law based on universal suffrage was promised.
10. The central government accepted the revolutionary regime's land reform program, but the agreement provided for compensation to private owners through a

joint commission representing the central government and the provincial council.[10]

Leftist elements in Tehran and Azerbaijan were overjoyed with the apparent concessions to their side. The most important points—land distribution, selection of the governor, armed forces, taxes, and parliamentary representation—had been solved in favor of the Azerbaijan regime. To the Soviets, the conclusion of the draft agreement was only an opening wedge for further concessions.

The agreement also increased Qavam's prestige and popularity. It proved to the populace that, without sacrificing the nation's territorial sovereignty, Qavam was able to negotiate effectively with the Russians and the Azerbaijani rebels. Furthermore, it gave the premier the necessary time to concentrate on other pressing matters, including preparations for elections to the Fifteenth Majlis.

Dr. Ali Shayegan, commenting on the agreement, stated:

> Qavam was a clever negotiator. He was successful because he was able to win the confidence of the Russians yet, at the same time, impress upon them that he was not interested in a settlement which was in violation of the Iranian constitution.[11]

Premier Qavam, taking advantage of his popularity, announced the formation of a new party on 29 June. The idea was inspired by the indefatigable Mozaffar Firouz, who convinced Qavam that the government could rely on neither the support of the Shah nor that of the Tudeh party. Thus it became urgent for Qavam to organize his own political organization. Its purposes were to demonstrate Qavam's support amongst the masses to the Shah and to contest the general elections which the Soviets and their supporters were anticipating impatiently. The organization was named the Democratic Party of Iran—a shrewd choice designed to steal the thunder of the Democratic Party of Azerbaijan.[12]

Qavam invited all classes to embrace the party and, using the vast resources of the government, the new party soon mounted a serious challenge to the parties of both the Right and the Left.

In order to fulfill one of the articles of the draft agreement Premier Qavam appointed Dr. Salamollah Javid, former minister of interior in Pishevari's government, as the governor-general for Azerbaijan. Javid was invited to Tehran to work on procedures for establishing the joint commissions and for implementing other articles of the agreement.

Javid met with the Shah on 7 July. Javid told the monarch that the Azerbaijan government did not want to separate from Iran, but to put an end to the corruption and the decadent bureaucracy of the central government. The Shah answered by praising the work of Javid and stating that his aim was also to rid the nation of the evils of a cumbersome bureaucracy.[13]

The Coalition Government

Qavam formed a coalition cabinet on 1 August 1946 that included three members of the Tudeh party—Dr. Fereidoun Keshavarz, minister of education; Iraj Eskandari, commerce and industry, and Dr. Morteza Yazdi, health. In addition, Allayar Saleh of the Iran Party* joined the cabinet as minister of justice, and Mozaffar Firouz became deputy-premier as well as minister of labor and propaganda.[14] Qavam's skillful maneuver was so swift that it took his cabinet, the Shah, and the country completely by surprise, but it served both to neutralize the Tudeh and to please the Soviet Union.

Qavam felt that he could better handle the Tudeh party inside the government than outside. He also wanted to use the power of the Tudeh among the trade unions to control the growing labor unrest that threatened the government's negoti-

* The Iran Party had worked out an agreement to collaborate with the Tudeh party.

ations with the Azerbaijan representatives. That the Tudeh role could be of importance had been demonstrated in the course of a general strike in Khuzistan on 14 July 1946.[15]

The strike had been carried out by Tudeh-backed unions, who protested against the low salaries paid by the Anglo-Iranian Oil Company and demanded the removal of the governor and the commander of troops of Khuzistan. As a result of the demonstrations in Abadan, the center of the oil refinery, twenty-four persons had been killed and 170 wounded. The British had dispatched naval reinforcements to the vicinity and had threatened intervention in case of danger to British lives and property. Iran had been faced with a major diplomatic crisis.[16]

Qavam dispatched a government commission headed by Mozaffar Firouz on 16 July. Included in the group were Dr. Reza Radmanesh, the Tudeh's general secretary, and Dr. Hussein Jowdat, a representative of the Tudeh labor union. They had persuaded the strikers to return to work by the promise of wage increases and the acceptance of the concept of collective bargaining by the Anglo-Iranian Oil Company. The governor and the commander of the troops in Khuzistan had been dismissed and Tudeh members who had been arrested were released.[17]

Mozaffar Firouz later described the situation:

I flew to Abadan and, after ordering all prisoners to be freed, I succeeded in putting an end to the strike. This helped turn back a British destroyer which had come into Iranian waters, with a view to landing troops on Iranian soil, on the pretext that British property and residents were in danger, which would have meant a new division (de facto), of Iran like 1907 with the Russians in the North and the British in the South. I gave them formal notification of the new labor code to the oil company and informed them officially that they would be obliged to pay the workers on a seven day basis for a six day week. When the head of the company replied that he would refer to London for instructions, I replied that the respect of Iranian laws by the company was imperative and no concern of London.[18]

Qavam also felt that the identification of the Tudeh party with the ruling class would help undermine the party's image as the champion of the masses and help improve the prestige of his own political party. The Tudeh contended that all the governments of Iran had been corrupt, effete, and hostile to the masses. It claimed that there could be no compromise between the party and the Iranian ruling class, but now its leaders were joining a cabinet whose members they had attacked time and again. They took an oath of allegiance to the Shah and an administration which they had denounced many times. This caused a wide cleavage within the party, with the left wing condemning the move and warning that it would nullify the revolutionary impact of the party.

The offer to participate in the government was so tempting to the Tudeh, however, that no serious deliberations were made before acceptance. Years later the decision was explained by the central committee of the party as an opportunity not only to safeguard the advantages already gained for the movement but also to prevent a reversal of the government's foreign policies. Furthermore, the party could thus strengthen the government's leftist trend and neutralize the Shah's pressure on the prime minister. The central committee claimed that this participation was not unconditional and had been made contingent on the acceptance of a democratic program of agrarian reform, the final solution of Azerbaijan, and free elections.[19]

The party also felt that by joining the cabinet it could help organize the majority of seats in the Fifteenth Majlis for the Communist movement. It was argued that while the Tudeh party was increasingly losing its revolutionary character and alienating the radical Left, it was offering the rank-and-file the prospect of seizing power through nonrevolutionary methods.

In anticipation of the elections the Soviets encouraged the Tudeh leaders to form an electoral popular front of parties of the Left and the Center. This was to include the prime minister's Democratic Party of Iran, the Iran party, and the three Communist parties—the Democratic Party of Azerbaijan, the Kurdish Kumeleh party, and the Tudeh party. The plan was to offer a single ticket in all electoral districts and to divide the seats by a proportional system. Events conspired, however, to put an end to this plan, or any other plan, and to topple the coalition government then in office.[20]

The Collapse of the Rebellion

The situation in Tehran caused the Western nations to adopt a more active approach. The new policy was spearheaded for the British by Sir John LeRougetel, who had replaced Sir Reader Bullard as ambassador, and by Ambassador George Allen for the United States. Both nations were aware that the popular front cabinet had many characteristics of classical communist penetration into the governing institutions of a non-Communist country.

The British perceived the Communist influence not only in Tehran but also in the southern areas, thus threatening their oil interest, the smooth running of the navy, and the security of the British empire.[21] The United States was more optimistic, as can be seen in the following telegram, which was sent by Ambassador Allen on 6 August 1946, to the secretary of state:

...Secretary Rossow [Robert], who was in Azerbaijan during development of puppet regime there, points out many similarities between sequence of events there and here, and thinks Qavam has already lost control of situation.

First stage in Azerbaijan was formation of Tudeh. Second was formation Democrats of Azerbaijan, which appeared to oppose Tudeh at start and consequently attracted considerable number fairly respectable followers on this basis. Third stage (which is one we are just entering in Tehran) was union of Tudeh and Democrats of Azerbaijan forces. Result was complete domination of government by better organized, financed, and supported Soviet agents.

Rossow feels situation in remainder of Iran has now gone so far, full Soviet domination of whole country is inevitable and Qavam could not retrieve situation, even if he exerted his utmost.

Many similarities between developments in Azerbaijan and those taking place in Tehran are evident. However, there are also differences which furnish basis for belief situation here is not irretrievably lost. Outstanding consideration is Qavam's continued support of Schwarzkopf Mission which is anathema to Tudeh Party. Moreover, there are no Russian speaking agents from Caucasus in high position there. Azerbaijan group established themselves in power behind Soviet bayonets but no such entrenchment of Tudeh has been possible here.

I regard situation as gloomy but by no means desperate.[22]

Meanwhile, negotiations with the Azerbaijan authorities had begun in Tehran in order to write the protocol for implementation of the Tabriz agreement. The meetings of the joint commission were chaired by Premier Qavam.

A major stumbling block was the military issue concerning the status of the Azerbaijani regular and volunteer forces. The Azerbaijanis proposed that:

1. The 160 Iranian officers who had deserted the national army and joined the Azerbaijan regular forces should receive legal recognition and be promoted two ranks higher than their rank at the time of desertion.

2. All other officers and noncommissioned officers who had been appointed by the Azerbaijan government should be accepted as the official officers of the Iranian army serving in Azerbaijan.

3. The central government should accept responsibility for the total budget of the Azerbaijan forces, but payments should be made through the government of Azerbaijan.
4. The commander in chief and all senior officers should receive the approval of the Azerbaijan provincial council.
5. Azerbaijan troops should not be transferred to any other areas without the approval of the provincial council.[23]

These proposals were opposed by the national army's high command. The Army chief of staff, Ali Razmara, argued energetically that if these proposals were accepted, "it would then lead to the dissolution of the Iranian army."[24] He further explained that there would be a revolt within the national army if the deserters and others who had rebelled against the central government were given official recognition and rewarded with promotions.

Ten long sessions were held in the presence of the prime minister, with the representatives of Azerbaijan and Mozaffar Firouz arguing for the acceptance of the proposals and the army high command opposing it. The premier and his cabinet worked hard for a compromise solution, but due to the rigid posture taken by the army leadership and the Azerbaijan government, their efforts reached an impasse.[25]

A State Department document reveals that on 25 August 1946, Qavam told Ambassador Allen that he was disappointed with his experiment of appointing Tudeh members to his cabinet. Explaining his view, Qavam said he "had hoped they would prove to be patriotic Iranians when they saw from the inside how [the] U.S.S.R. was treating Iran every day but they continued to follow the Soviet line."[26] Qavam also said the Tudeh party was clearly directed by the Soviet Embassy and that he was searching for a good basis for throwing its members out of the cabinet."[27]

It is interesting to note that during this time, high Iranian officials were directly involved with the American ambassador without the knowledge of Premier Qavam. In the 25 August communique George Allen reported to the secretary of state:

> Conversations with Azerbaijans (sic), will continue for several days. So far only military matters have been discussed but today equally difficult financial questions will be on the agenda. Bank Melli Director Ebtehaj telephoned this morning just before conference with Azerbaijans (sic), to find out Prime Minister's mood and to repeat his own determination to remain absolutely firm against Azerbaijan demands. My general impression is that Qavam is very reluctant to resort to other than conciliatory means with Azerbaijan but that in the end he will use force.[28]

The following secret message sent by Ambassador Allen to the secretary of state on 6 September 1946 is also very instructive:

> During conversation with Prime Minister yesterday subject turned to oil, which Qavam considers chief Soviet aim in Iran. If USSR can obtain its desires both as regards oil and Azerbaijan it will do so but, if forced to choose between the two, he feels confident Soviets will drop Azerbaijan.[29]

For Premier Qavam this assumption was to form the foundation of his future strategy in dealing with the Azerbaijan question.

Mozaffar Firouz went to Isfahan on 8 September where he ordered the arrest of the Bakhtiari chiefs including Morteza Qoli Khan and his sons. It was announced that an antigovernment plot was being prepared by the British for the rising of the Bakhtiari and Qashqai tribes, with a view to capturing Isfahan and forming a "reactionary, feudal, tribal government."[30]

Prince Firouz later recalled, "after sacking the governor of the town, I asked for the removal of the British Consul whose letters to certain tribal leaders had fallen in my hands."[31] The Bakhtiari chiefs were sent to Tehran and a military governor was appointed for the region.

The British, alarmed by the extension of Soviet power into the government and southward, were contemplating a move away from the American position toward a compromise with the Russians. The British reasoned that the continued efforts of the Iranian government to consider Azerbaijan part of Iran was contrary to reality and had created a desperate situation in which there was no clear-cut frontier between the Soviet Union and Iran. Under such conditions the Soviets would be free to continue their infiltration of Tehran and to exert more pressure on the southern region, thus endangering the vital interests of the British.

Moreover, the British felt Qavam should agree to sever Azerbaijan from Iran and establish strong military forces along the Irano-Azerbaijan border. This action would then enable Tehran to better resist Soviet-inspired demands in the rest of the country—such as the inclusion of Tudeh members in the cabinet and other conciliatory measures the government had been making in the struggle to keep Azerbaijan as part of the nation.[32]

To this end, the British moved vigorously to consolidate their position in the south and to pressure Qavam into breaking with the Tudeh and the Azerbaijan government.

United States Ambassador George Allen disagreed with the British position. On 28 September 1946, in a secret communique to the secretary of state, Allen declared:

> I am inclined to believe that severance of Azerbaijan would not in fact relieve Soviet pressure on rest of country and might well place USSR merely in stronger position to realize other aims. Nor am I ready to admit that Azerbaijan has been irreparably lost, even though its recovery seems remote at the moment. Moreover, while I realize that present national boundaries of Iran, which result from historical accident or ancient conquests, are not sacred and

that Azerbaijans (sic), may be closer in language and feelings to Turks in Turkey and USSR than to Iran, it seems to me we have no alternative but to continue to support integrity of Iran in accordance with Declaration Regarding Iran and United Nations Charter.[33]

An open tribal rebellion broke out in Fars on 20 September. The Qashqai tribe, under the leadership of Nasser Khan and Khusrow Khan, protested against the influence of Communists in the government. The Bakhtiaris and several minor tribes from Fars, Khuzistan, and the Gulf coast joined in the uprising.

After the capture of Bushire and Abadeh, the provincial governor of Fars arrived in Tehran with a list of demands which the tribal leaders and religious and municipal authorities opposed to the Tudeh had drawn up in Shiraz, the provincial capital. They demanded the removal of the Tudeh ministers from the cabinet, the release of the Bakhtiari chiefs whom Firouz had arrested, and the same degree of provincial autonomy that had been granted to Azerbaijan in June.[34] Whatever the degree of the central government's complicity in this incident, Qavam exploited it in favor of a return to pre-coalition policies.

The British Foreign Office denied reports emanating from Tehran and Moscow that British ships in the Gulf were supplying the rebellious tribes with arms and ammunition.[35] The diplomatic correspondent of the London *Daily Worker* reported the following:

Long and carefully laid British plans to detach the oilfields from Persia and incorporate them in Iraq appear to be maturing. The tribesmen who have seized ports on the Persian Gulf are well armed, and it was not their own government which provided them with sub-machine guns, rifles and ammunition. . . .It is known that representatives of these tribes have recently made visits to Basra, where British H.Q. is situated. . . .An atmosphere of tension is being deliberately built-up—just the atmosphere in which it will be possible for the British to carry out their threat to send troops across the frontier to 'protect British lives and property.'[36]

The Iranian ambassador to London asked the Foreign Office to investigate an accusation that Alan Charles Trott, the British consul-general at Ahwaz, and C. A. Gault, consul-general at Isfahan, had incited the southern tribes to rebel; and despite categorical denial by the Foreign Office of complicity, the Iranian government persisted for a time in its request for the removal of the two officials.[37]

An editorial in *Rahbar*, the organ of the Tudeh party, criticized those who were trying to equate the revolt in the South with that of the Azerbaijan revolution. It stated that while the goals of the revolution in Azerbaijan were to achieve equality and freedom for the peasants and workers, who for years were oppressed by Reza Shah's dictatorship, the rebellion in the South was led by feudal leaders supported by British imperialists.

The editorial also argued that it was deceptive to link parliamentary elections to the settlement of the Azerbaijan problem. It claimed that "the leaders of the Azerbaijan movement have stated many times their willingness to cooperate with the government of Iran, but the postponement of the elections and the tribal revolt confirms the fact that Qavam is not interested in a parliamentary democracy but wants to continue the present period of interregnum."[38]

The rebellion continued to spread, and the Iranian army surrendered Kazirun to the rebels. The government was forced to negotiate with the tribal leaders and eventually to concede most of their demands.

Meanwhile, S. I. Sychev, chief of the Middle Eastern Division of the Soviet Foreign Ministry, had arrived in Tehran to press Qavam for a speedy ratification of the oil agreement.

It was officially announced on 6 October that the Shah had signed the decree for elections to the Fifteenth Majlis, although there was still considerable discussion about when they should begin. The Left was calling for speed, but the conservatives urged postponement on account of the unsettled conditions in the provinces.[39]

On the same date Ambassador Allen sent the following urgent message to the secretary of state:

> Shah said last night he had just signed decree calling for immediate preparations for elections. He does not know exact date elections will be held but presumes they will take place in 'about a month.' He hesitated to sign decree in view of disturbed state of country but decided he should not assume responsibility for further delay.
>
> Shah is afraid parliament to be elected will be divided between outright Soviet spokesmen and deputies loyal to Qavam. He thinks latter group will also be susceptible to heavy Soviet pressure and that consequently new parliament will 'end Iranian independence' unless strong action is taken beforehand. He is toying with idea of asking Qavam to resign to enable formation of interim government to conduct elections. Announced basis for Shah's action would be that Qavam, who is leader of political party, should not conduct elections in which his party is a contestant. Real basis for Shah's concern is his fear that new parliament, elected under control of Qavam and Muzzafar Firuz,* would be hostile to him and western democracies.
>
> In response to Shah's request for advice I said decision was one no foreigner had right to suggest and he must decide with his own counselors. . . .
>
> I am unable to guess Shah's probable action but suspect he may end by doing nothing, which may be best in circumstances. I have frequently cautioned him during conversations regarding Qavam that he should consider carefully the alternative. If he should force out present cabinet and substitute for it reactionary regime regarded by Iranians as British stooges result will be shortlived. I am confident British themselves would not welcome such a regime. On

---

* Ambassador Allen uses a different spelling for the name of Mozaffar Firouz.

other hand, there is real danger that new parliament elected under present government may be Soviet-dominated. On balance I am inclined to let matters take their course. . . .[40]

Pressure mounted on Qavam to reorganize his cabinet and drop the Tudeh ministers. The newspaper *Peykar*, in an editorial, stated that "the people of Iran are reminding the prime minister that the inclusion of the Tudeh members in the cabinet was based on the assumption that with their help, it could lead to the settlement of the Azerbaijan crisis. Not only the Azerbaijan revolt has not been resolved but to it must be added the rebellion in the South. Therefore, the time has come for the formation of a strong, independent cabinet, which would more effectively put an end to the revolutions in Azerbaijan and Fars provinces."[41]

The United States government also increased its pressure on Qavam. It felt that the situation in Iran was so critical that everything had to be done to prevent Iran from slipping into the Soviet orbit. For the United States, the preservation of Iranian sovereignty was a matter of political and strategic interest. Explaining this view, the Joint Chiefs of Staff held that the strategic interests of the United States would be greatly harmed by the division of Iran into spheres of influence, or if that nation should fall completely under Soviet domination. They felt that the oil fields of Iran, Saudi Arabia, and Iraq were absolutely vital to the security of the United States.[42]

On 12 October Ambassador Allen reported to the secretary of state that he had brought the following situation to the attention of the Iranian prime minister:

Immediately after a recent cabinet meeting discussing the aviation agreement with the Soviet Union, a member of the cabinet had informed the Soviet Embassy of the exact position taken by each member and that within 24 hours a

Soviet official had demanded of a cabinet member why he had opposed Soviet interests. . . .that 'when such conditions existed, it was obvious that present Government of Iran had no freedom or independence and that we might as well recognize the fact and cease pretending."[43]

Qavam resigned with other members of the government on 17 October 1946, and, in the new cabinet which he formed on 19 October the three Communist ministers were dropped. Because of heavy pressure from the Shah, Mozaffar Firouz was also excluded from the cabinet and was instead appointed ambassador to Moscow.

State Department documents show that during a meeting with Ambassador Allen on 19 October 1946, the Shah explained that he had given the following instructions to Qavam on the morning of 17 October:

. . .that both Firuzes and three Tudeh members must be dismissed from cabinet and Qavam's party must fight Tudeh with all its strength during coming election. Nothing further must be heard of coalition with Tudeh or collaboration. . .regarding election.[44]

Ambassador Allen further reported:

Qavam promptly agreed to everything except dismissal of Muzzafar Firuz, pleading to keep him or, at least, for short while. Shah says he became furious, banged table, and told Qavam that mention of Firuz again would end any cooperation between himself and Qavam forever. Shah said he wanted Firuz either in prison or out of country immediately. Qavam suggested sending him to Moscow and Shah agreed provided it was done immediately. . .[45]

George Allen also sent the following secret message to the secretary of state regarding the changes in Qavam's cabinet:

. . .new cabinet is primarily straight Qavam Party government, in contrast to previous coalition government. Its formation has resulted from combination of circumstances, but primarily from realization by Qavam that collaboration with Tudeh was not possible. My representation to Qavam on October 11th regarding loss of independence of his government and British Ambassador's insistent advice and warning against collaboration with Tudeh in forthcoming elections have helped bring about decision. Tudeh cabinet members angered Qavam by truculent attitude they took against settlement of Fars revolt and by inordinate demands they made for control of forthcoming Majlis. Soviet Ambassador overplayed his hand and used threatening tone in recent conversations with Qavam. These and other considerations have convinced Qavam that his efforts to maintain coalition government could not continue and that he must make a clear-cut break with Tudeh. He will try to avoid open break with Moscow, and Muzzafar Firuz is slated to go to Moscow as Ambassador.

I do not believe Tudeh party will accept Qavam's decision quietly. . . .All Qavam's powers of manipulation will be needed to prevent Azerbaijan from breaking into armed hostilities. Soviet reaction against him will probably be violent, in spite of his efforts to conciliate USSR.

New cabinet is very considerable improvement over former one. It is fortunate that change came about on Qavam's own initiative since serious difficulties, which would have arisen if Shah had had to force change on Qavam, have been avoided.[46]

The new cabinet was centrist, excluded right-wing representatives, and was made up primarily of independent and nationalist elements. This was a serious blow to the Tudeh party. In retrospective "self-criticism," Iraj Eskandari, who was a member in the short-lived coalition government, wrote in *Moyen-Orient* that if the party and other democratic organizations had succeeded in imposing a general election on Qavam at the beginning of 1946, this setback would have been avoided; but by wishfully thinking that the prime minister would honor his commitment under the Iranian-Soviet draft agreement and hold elections soon, and by overestimating the personal differences separating Qavam and the Shah, the democratic movement lost a precious opportunity.[47]

Mozaffar Firouz, in an answer to a question concerning the role of the Tudeh in the coalition cabinet, stated:

It was on my personal initiative and insistence that Qavam accepted their entry into the government. My object in bringing them into the government was to give them a sense of responsibility and test them in action. I proposed to the Tudeh that we form a large popular front with a programme of action covering ten years in order to completely transform Iran politically and economically and by the active participation of our youth give the country modern democratic institutions. I insisted that all communist and ideological talk must be set aside for the ten year period and all attention and energy given to the execution of the programme. Unfortunately I found no sense of statesmanship amongst the Tudeh leaders and the party was full of British agents who sabotaged any plan of real action and for this reason a great historical opportunity for the democratic forces of the country was lost.[48]

In an interview, Dr. Ali Shayegan expressed the same opinion. Answering a question on the Qasqai revolt, Shayegan said, "Qavam was happy to use the Qasqai rebellion to get rid of the Tudeh deputies. The Tudeh ministers were too arrogant and felt that they were there forever. Their arrogance brought on their downfall."[49]

In another interview, Nasser Khan Qasqai, the head of the Qasqai tribe, disclosed the following:

We revolted because we feared a Communist takeover of Iran. We opposed both the British and the Russians. Our aim was a united Iran.

We felt that the Azerbaijan rebellion was not a nationalist movement but was controlled and directed by the Soviet Union.

We demanded the removal of the Tudeh ministers from the cabinet. Our main point was that if the Russians would annex northern Iran, at least with the Tudeh out of the cabinet, the government could move swiftly to save the Capital.

The British liked our movement but were not dictating to us and we were not under their control. They took advantage of the situation.

If Qavam had listened to Mozaffar Firouz, they could have easily ousted the Shah.[50]

As soon as news of the resignation of Qavam and the dropping of Firouz and the three Tudeh members was revealed in Tehran, Pishevari's representatives, who were negotiating the implementation of the Tabriz agreement, broke off their meetings and left for Tabriz.[51]

This serious blow to the Tudeh party led to a major struggle with Qavam's supporters, causing the loss of strength for both sides. It was the Shah, backed by the army and by the United States, who began to emerge as the dominant force in Iran.

Bitterness among the Tudeh grew as the government followed up the dissolution of the coalition cabinet with a major reversal of policy toward the Communist movement, including an unwillingness to tolerate labor agitation as an instrument of pressure. A strike by a Tudeh-sponsored union on 12 November provided an excuse for the wholesale arrest of hundreds of trade union members and leading party functionaries in Tehran and the rest of the country.[52]

Confident that Soviet interest in an early convening of the new Majlis would prevent serious objections from Moscow, Qavam next resolved to make the presence of Iranian army units in Azerbaijan a prerequisite for holding elections. To allay Soviet misgivings that the new Majlis might take a hostile attitude toward the April agreement, he endeavored to give every appearance of intending to participate actively in the elections in all constituencies and to win a majority for his party, which would fully support his commitments.[53]

Accordingly, it was announced in Tehran that elections would begin on 7 December, and on 21 November Qavam

stated that "in order to ensure freedom of voting and to sup-
press possible disturbances" they would be held under the
supervision of government forces throughout the country.[54]

Ambassador Allen actively supported Premier Qavam in
these actions and advised the State Department that it was in
the best interests of the United States not to oppose the elections. Allen cabled:

> Decision as to best course is difficult, but I still believe our
> best policy is not to assume responsibility ourselves for op-
> posing elections. Shah and others who favor postponement
> but who do not have nerve enough to say so openly, would
> like nothing better than to be able to say United States has
> advised against them, in order to turn Soviet blasts against
> United States. Soviets would say United States was trying
> to block Soviet oil concession.[55]

On 22 November 1946, encouraged by assurances of a more
active American policy in support of the territorial sovereignty
of Iran*—and also after a conference with the Shah, the
minister of war, and the army chief of staff—Qavam ordered
the minister of war to dispatch troops to Zanjan and Azerbaijan. At the same time, the agents of the central government
encouraged the Shahsavan tribes of Azerbaijan and the Zoulfaqari brothers** of Zanjan to start a revolt. The Democrats
of Zanjan showed no resistance and escaped from the area before the detachments of troops arrived from Tehran.[56]

Following violent protests from Tabriz, the United States
ambassador, George V. Allen, was asked the following question by a reporter from the newspaper *Ettelaat*:

---

* A State Department document reveals that on November 14, 1946, the United
States Government had agreed in principle to sell to the Iranian army and gendarmerie (Brigadier-General Schwarzkopf was this time still serving as the
gendarmerie's advisor), reasonable quantities of military supplies for the purpose of
maintaining internal security.
** Zoulfaqari brothers—Nasser, Mohammed, and Mahmud—were feudal
landlords who owned most of the land in the Zanjan area.

What is your opinion regarding the recent decision of the Government of Iran to send security forces to various parts of Iran, including Azerbaijan, in connection with the forthcoming elections?[57]

Ambassador Allen answered:

It is the well-known policy of the American Government to favor the maintenance of Iranian sovereignty and territorial integrity. This principle was stated in the Declaration Regarding Iran signed at Tehran, December 1, 1943, and is embodied in the principles of the United Nations Charter. The announced intention of the Iranian Government to send its security forces into all parts of Iran, including any areas of Iran where such forces are not at present in control, for the maintenance of order in connection with the elections, seems to me an entirely normal and proper decision.[58]

On the same day, the Soviet ambassador left his sickbed to protest to the Shah and Premier Qavam against the government's "unfriendly policy," and to warn that the Soviet Union could not "look with favor on bloodshed in Azerbaijan." He reminded the Premier of the still-pending oil agreement, but Qavam's action had cleverly presented the Soviet Union with two mutually exclusive alternatives: either having a Majlis elected as a preliminary to the submission of the oil agreement for ratification, or maintaining the Communist regime in Azerbaijan at the price of an indefinite postponement of ratification. To achieve both alternatives it would have been necessary to invade Iran again, or at least to threaten an invasion.[59] Russian foreign policy in general had recently become more conciliatory, a change which was plausibly ascribed both to the resistance which the United States had shown to her aggressive demonstrations since the end of the war and to internal difficulties arising from the reconstruction of her war-ravaged economy.[60]

Qavam meanwhile instructed Hussein Ala to inform the Security Council that the Soviet ambassador, Ivan Sadchikov, had given "friendly admonition" at Tehran that the movement of the Iranian troops into Azerbaijan might result in disturbances within that province and on the Iranian borders adjacent to the Soviet Union.[61]

Ala, in a letter to Herschel V. Johnson, president of the Security Council, made it clear that Sadchikov had advised the Iranian government to abandon the plan and called this an infringement of the sovereign rights of an independent state, contrary to the spirit and letter of the Charter of the United Nations. Ala further stated, "no request for action is made at the present time, though it will be apparent that the decision of the Security Council to continue seized of this question should remain unchanged."[62]

At the same time, Qavam rejected a suggestion by the Azerbaijan Provincial Council that the central government content itself with sending inspectors and press correspondents to watch the conduct of the elections by the provincial authorities and instead ordered government troops to continue their advance from Zanjan. In reply, Tabriz radio announced that the Provincial government had distributed arms to all workers, members of the national militia, and youth associations, and had made a rousing declaration that they would defend the republic with the last drop of their blood.[63]

While central government aircraft scattered leaflets exhorting the people of Azerbaijan to overthrow the Democrats of Azerbaijan, a note assured the Soviet Embassy that the intended action was merely for the purpose of supervising the elections and was in no way directed against Soviet interests. It was observed in Moscow that the Soviet press was commenting on the Azerbaijan crisis as a purely Iranian matter, "with a certain air of detachment."[64]

Iranian troops crossed the provincial border on 10 December 1946, meeting with only slight resistance from the ill-equipped and undisciplined opposing forces. On 12

December the army entered Tabriz, and within a few days the insurrection in Azerbaijan and Kurdistan collapsed. The top leaders, including Pishevari, escaped to the Soviet Union, but most members of the lower echelon were captured. Some of the active leaders, including the rebellious officers of the central government, paid with their lives. Others died in the riots and clashes between royalist tribes and pro-Communist elements in the days between the capitulation and the restoration of order by government forces.[65]

American and British correspondents who arrived in Tabriz on 12 December reported that the populace eagerly awaited the approach of government troops and greeted them as liberators.[66]

The Iranian central authorities now set about eradicating all traces of the autonomist regime of Azerbaijan. Students were reported to have destroyed textbooks written in the local Turkish dialect which the Democrats had provided them, and *Farsi* once again became the language of Tabriz radio and the local press.[67]

In Tehran the government adopted some very harsh measures against the Tudeh party. Its headquarters were occupied by the military authorities, its newspapers suppressed, and many of its leaders were thrown into prison. The triumph of the government was complete. Azerbaijan was united with the rest of the country exactly a year after the rebellion, and the Tudeh party was reduced to impotence in the capital.

In Moscow the Soviets criticized the leaders of the Azerbaijan rebellion for not compromising their differences with the central government.[68] Again in retrospective "self-criticism," the Tudeh leadership sought to explain the Azerbaijan collapse on the grounds that "the militant peasants were so dispersed and unorganized that their indispensable alliance with the working class could not yet be realized, while the working class itself. . .did not have the necessary cohesion and political training to play effectively its role of leader in the revolutionary movements."[69]

It was therefore after a careful examination that the Provincial Assembly of Azerbaijan met in the presence of party leaders in an extraordinary session on 12 December and resolved to issue a cease-fire. This "grave decision" was based on "rigorous revolutionary logic," for continued resistance would have resulted in direct intervention by the imperialist powers in Iran, "bringing the war to the immediate frontiers of the Soviet Union and constituting a grave danger for world peace and security." It was also later admitted that the cease-fire was a tactical mistake, for the immediate withdrawal of the Azerbaijani forces turned into a disorganized route.[70]

The End of the Oil Controversy

The contrast between conditions in 1947 and those of 1946 could hardly have been greater. Soviet influence had completely receded, for Qavam had successfully exploited the wide differences that existed between the former allies in the war against Germany. The Soviets could not have intervened to prevent the Iranian reoccupation of Azerbaijan without an open invasion, which would have called down the wrath of the Western powers gathered around the Security Council table. The tactic was changed to that of maintaining strong pressure through the channels of diplomacy in order to further the immediate Russian aim in Iran, namely parliamentary ratification of a petroleum concession in the northern territories. Meanwhile American influence was rapidly reaching its height. Military and economic aid was increased, and promises were made of further financial assistance.[71]

At the same time, Qavam's clever handling of the Azerbaijan crisis had greatly increased his prestige. The position of the Shah and the army, as a point around which the nation could rally, was also strengthened. This was more remarkable when it was remembered what a blow the Iranian army had received to its prestige in 1941 and the widespread unpopularity which had attached to it as an institution during Reza Shah's regime.

In January 1947, procedures for the long-delayed parliamentary elections began. During the campaign, a major struggle developed between the candidates supported by Qavam and those backed by the Shah. The Shah, suspicious of Qavam and working through the army, wanted to elect representatives to the Majlis who were loyal to him. Qavam, relying on his power as prime minister and leader of the Democratic party, was seeking to monopolize the elections to his advantage.[72]

Newspapers subsidized by the Shah openly attacked Premier Qavam. On 4 January 1947, the newspaper *Javan Mardom* published an editorial accusing Qavam of initiating a plan to depose the Shah and establish a republic. The article stated that Qavam had secretly conspired with the Soviet Union and the Tudeh party to overthrow the monarchy by electing all his supporters to the Majlis. A Majlis packed with Qavam's adherents would then depose the Shah and elect Qavam president. The editorial called on the army to take all necessary action to end the premier's "sinister plotting."

Supporters of Qavam attacked the courtiers around the Shah for their interference in the elections and accused them of undermining the actions of the government. The conflict intensified during the months of January and February, and the Shah openly instructed Qavam not to interfere with the elections. Backers of Qavam and the Shah clashed in the streets.[73] Dr. Mussadeq attacked the old pattern of imperial intervention in a speech and called on both the Shah and Qavam to cease their heavy-handed interference.[74]

By the end of June, elections were finally completed. Qavam's Democratic party won a substantial majority of seats, but this meant little in the flexible state of Iranian politics. The opposition led by Dr. Mussadeq counted about

twenty-five deputies. Another group of twenty represented the
Shah. The Tudeh party, defeated and disorganized, had boycotted the elections.[75]

The class composition of the Majlis was fifty percent upper-
class landowners, thirty-five percent big businessmen and urban merchants, fifteen percent intellectuals, journalists, and
university professors.[76] In one aspect, this newly elected
Majlis differed from that of the Fourteenth Majlis. A large
number of independent, strong-willed intellectuals were
elected to the Fourteenth Majlis, including members of the
Tudeh party. In the Fifteenth Majlis only a small group of
intellectuals and university professors was elected, and many
deputies of the previous Majlis had been forbidden by Qavam
and the Shah to take part in the elections.

It became obvious that the majority, elected under arranged conditions and desirous of protecting their class
interest, were anti-Soviet. In fact, the viewpoint of most could
be predicted, except on the question of how long they would
stay loyal to Qavam in the face of the constant intrigues of the
Shah and his court.

The procedure for organizing the Majlis, electing its officers, and examining the credentials of its members was
taking its leisurely course through the hot summer days when,
on 12 August 1947, the Soviet ambassador presented Qavam
with the text of an oil agreement for his signature. Qavam
refused to sign until it had been presented and approved by
the Majlis.[77]

The Russians pressed hard for action on ratification. On 25
August and 15 September Sadchikov handed additional notes
to Premier Qavam in which he accused him of delaying tactics
and called his policy a return to the old hostility and inde-
fensible discrimination against the Soviet Union pursued by
Reza Shah and previous governments.[78]

A divergence was beginning to appear between British and
American policy concerning Iran. The British government

was apprehensive lest outright rejection of the Soviet demand for the joint development of the oil resources of northern Iran lead to the elimination of the British concession in the south. Britain could only hope to retain this if she had the pretext of a corresponding Soviet concession in the north. Therefore, the British ambassador, Sir John Le Rougetel, was instructed to hand Qavam a note which recommended that "the Persian Government might be well advised to leave the door open for further discussions. . . .If they could not accept the Soviet draft treaty—they might leave opportunity for revised and fairer terms to be presented."[79]

In the midst of mounting Iranian suspicion that Britain, the Soviet Union, and perhaps the United States had reached an agreement at Iran's expense, Ambassador Allen issued a strong and candid statement. On 11 September, speaking to the Irano-American Cultural Relations Society, the Ambassador declared:

> Certain rumors and allegations have appeared concerning the attitude of the United States in this matter, and I have been asked to state my Government's position.
>
> The American Government has frequently made known its respect for Iran's sovereignty. An important aspect of sovereignty is the full right of any country to accept or reject proposals for the development of its resources. Iran's resources belong to Iran. Iran can give them away free of charge, or refuse to dispose of them at any price, if it so desires. . .
>
> The United States is firm in its conviction that any proposals made by one sovereign government to another should not be accompanied by threats or intimidation. When such methods are used in an effort to gain acceptance, doubt is cast on the value of the proposals. . .[80]

The Ambassador went on to affirm the American position in a manner which Iranian opinion was bound to interpret as full encouragement to reject the Soviet proposals outright:

The United States has dedicated its full energy and resources to freeing the peoples of the world from the fear of aggression. Our determination to follow this policy is as strong as regards Iran as it is anywhere else in the world. Patriotic Iranians, when considering matters affecting their national interest, may therefore rest assured that the American people will support fully their freedom to make their own choice.[81]

Ambassador Allen's remarks must be interpreted not as an isolated outburst of American support toward Iran, but as part of a policy which had gradually developed in 1946 during the Irano-Soviet dispute over Azerbaijan and which was given concrete expression on 13 April 1947, in the Truman Doctrine regarding Greece and Turkey. In that statement the American president had called for a policy of containment of Communism throughout the world and had pledged the support of the American government to the defense of all small nations against aggression and infiltration.

The consequences of the energetic American support were felt in Iran immediately. In a series of forceful speeches before the Majlis, deputies attacked the Qavam-Sadchikov agreement as harmful and its signing by Qavam as illegal and unconstitutional.

On 21 September, the deputy, Abdul Hussein Etebar, attacked both the proposed Soviet Oil concession and the existing British one.[82] A week later, in a move which was seen as a sign that the government was leaning in the direction of opposing ratification, Ibrahim Khaje Nuri, deputy to the prime minister, appealed in a broadcast for purely national control of the oil resources.

Qavam presented his government and its general program to the Majlis on 5 October, but made no mention of oil. He received a vote of confidence of ninety-three to twenty-seven.[83] On 22 October, Qavam appeared before the Majlis to make a lengthy report of his negotiations with Russia. He denied charges by the opposition that he had signed an agreement with the Soviet Union. He contended that what he had signed was subject to the ratification of the Majlis. Qavam then presented his accord with Sadchikov to the Majlis and told the deputies that he was neither supporting nor opposing the concession but wanted the Majlis to study the whole situation dispassionately and to avoid any hasty action.[84]

Opposition to the agreement was led by Dr. Reza Zadeh Shafaq. He pointed out that the world situation had changed and that since many nations were either denouncing or modifying their past economic and commercial concessions, it was therefore unbecoming of a socialist nation like the Soviet Union to follow in the footsteps of the imperialist-capitalists by demanding an oil concession from Iran.[85]

Dr. Shafaq, after assuring the Soviet Union that no foreign corporation would develop the oil of northern Iran, introduced a bill which was adopted at the same session by a vote of 102 to 2. The first article of the law rejected the Qavam-Sadchikov agreement, but exonerated the prime minister by assuming that he had entered into discussions with Sadchikov by virtue of the second article of Dr. Mussadeq's law of 2 December 1944.[86]

Shafaq's bill provided for the following:

1. The Majlis considered Qavam's negotiations with the Soviet Union null and void but he would be exempted from the penalties provided by the law of 2 December 1944, against any minister who should negotiate oil concessions with foreigners.

2. The Iranian government during the next five years would explore and develop her own oil resources with Iranian capital. Should it be found necessary to engage foreign experts, they would be drawn from completely neutral countries.

3. The Iranian government would not grant oil concessions to foreign powers or take foreigners into partnership in any oil company.

4. If oil were found in the North of Iran, the government would be permitted to enter into discussions with the Soviet government in connection with the sale of oil products to that government but would have to keep the Majlis informed throughout.

5. The government was charged with undertaking such negotiations and measures in all cases where Iran's right to its natural resources, whether subterranean or otherwise, especially in the case of the oil resources in the southern part of the country, had been impaired; and making certain that all national rights should be restored. The government was further charged with informing the Majlis of the results of such negotiations and measures.[87]

The action of the Majlis brought several protests from the Soviet government. The Russian notes were curt but not uncompromising and made a particular point of the continued existence of the British oil concession in the South. These messages were accompanied by a propaganda campaign directed against the Iranian government by the Soviet press and Radio Moscow.

The nationalist fervor of the Majlis had been so inflamed that Qavam began to despair of his authority over it. In response to pressure from the opposition, Qavam started negotiations with the Anglo-Iranian Oil Company calling for revision of the 1933 agreement and a new arrangement for sharing profits between the government of Iran and the company. The British resisted Qavam, and the Americans abandoned him. The Shah worked effectively to undermine Qavam's power amongst the members of his cabinet and that of the Majlis. The opportunists moved to support the Shah.[88]

On 1 December, after summoning a secret session of the Majlis and failing to obtain a quorum, Qavam broadcast to the nation a warning that Iran should remain neutral between the two great power blocs. He also stated, "I have pursued the case of the Anglo-Iranian Oil Company concession and will persist as long as necessary to secure satisfaction for the Iranian nation." This appeal to nationalist sentiment did not save him. Astute as Qavam was at negotiating difficult political tangles, this one proved too much for him.[89]

The day after the broadcast most members of his cabinet resigned. A week later Qavam tried to form a new cabinet, but on 10 December 1947, after failing to receive a vote of confidence from the Majlis, he also resigned.[90]

Qavam's downfall was followed by riots and demonstrations typical of Iranian politics. Most of his friends and appointees in the Majlis and the country turned against him. The headquarters of his party were occupied by a mob, and Qavam, after being temporarily placed under arrest, was allowed to leave for Europe for medical reasons.

The problem of his successor was not an easy one. Four days later the post was offered by a vote of 72 out of 106 to Sardar Fakher Hekmat, the speaker of the Majlis. Dr. Mussadeq received thirty-one votes. Hekmat was unable to form a cabinet, and the Majlis next elected Ibrahim Hakimi who received fifty-four votes against Dr. Mussadeq's fifty-three.[91]

Hakimi, seventy-seven years old and a close friend of the court, was commissioned by the Shah to form a new government. He succeeded in putting together a cabinet, and for the next year or two Iranian politics resumed its familiar course. Governments rose and fell; reforms were promised and never carried out. American aid steadily grew more lavish and more all-embracing, while the Soviet Union grumbled openly but not very effectively at every fresh development.

The vote of the Majlis and the resignation of Qavam re-emphasized the failure of Soviet post-war policy in Iran, a general analysis of which is detailed in the next chapter.

Notes

1. Radmanesh, "Dar Bareh Nehzat 21 Azar" [About the 21st of Azar Movement], *Donya*, vol. 6, no. 4, (winter 1966), p. 12.

2. General Hassan Arfa, *Under Five Shahs* (New York: William Morrow and Co., 1965), p. 367.

3. Ibid., p. 366.

4. Department of State, *Foreign Relations of the United States, the Near East and Africa, 1946*, vol. 7, (Washington: Government Printing Office, 1969), pp. 438-39 (hereafter cited as *Foreign Relations of the United States*).

5. Presentation of Prince Mozaffar Firouz, Paris, 30 May 1969.

6. *New York Times*, 23 April 1946.

7. Najafgoli, *Marg Bud Bazgast Ham Bud* [These were both death and retreat] (Tehran: 1949), pp. 211-12 (hereafter cited as *Death and Retreat*).

8. Ibid.

9. Firouz (Presentation), Paris, 30 May 1969.

10. The Ministry of Labor and Propaganda, "Iran Dar Rah Eslahat Democratic" [Iran at the threshold of democratic reforms] (Tehran: 1946), pp. 100-103.

11. Interview with Dr. Ali Shayegan who was appointed minister of education in the cabinet formed by Qavam in October 1946, New York City, 15 November 1972.

12. *Khandaniha*, 12 July 1946; Firouz (Presentation), Paris, 30 May 1969.

13. *Khandaniha*, 12 July 1946.

14. Kambakhsh, *Nazari Be Jumbesh Kargari Va Communistry Dar Iran* [A glance at the Communist Labor Movement in Iran](Publication of the Tudeh Party of Iran, 1972), pp. 159-60 (hereafter cited as *Communist Labor Movement*).

15. Sephr Zabih, *The Communist Movement in Iran* (Berkeley: University of California Press, 1966), p. 113 (hereafter cited as *The Communist Movement*).

16. Ibid.; *Mehr-Iran*, 21 July 1946.

17. *Mehr-Iran*, 21 July 1946.

18. Firouz (Presentation), Paris, 30 May 1969.

19. Eskandari, *Moyen-Orient*, no. 11; as quoted in Zabih, *The Communist Movement*, p. 111-12.

20. Ibid., p. 114.

21. *Setareh*, 5 August 1946.

22. *Foreign Relations of the United States*, pp. 510-11.

23. *Pesyan, Death and Retreat*, pp. 219-20.

24. Ibid., p. 221.

25. Ibid., p. 223.

26. *Foreign Relations of the United States*, p. 513.

27. Ibid.

28. Ibid.

29. Ibid., p. 514.

30. *Setareh*, 11 September 1946.

31. Firouz (Presentation), Paris, 30 May 1969.

32. *Foreign Relations of the United States*, p. 517.

33. Ibid., p. 518.

34. George Kirk, *The Middle East in the War, Survey of International Affairs, 1939-46.* 3 vols. (London: Oxford University Press, 1952), 3:77-78 (hereafter cited as *The Middle East*).

35. *New York Times,* 24 September 1946.

36. *Daily Worker* (London), 24 September 1946.

37. Kirk, *The Middle East,* 3: 77-78.

38. *Rahbar,* 26 September 1946.

39. Kirk, *The Middle East,* 3: 79.

40. *Foreign Relations of the United States,* pp. 522-23.

41. *Peykar,* 5 October 1946.

42. *Foreign Relations of the United States,* p. 524.

43. Ibid., p. 537.

44. Ibid., p. 538.

45. Ibid.

46. Ibid., 19 October 1946, pp. 536-37.

47. Eskandari, *Moyen-Orient,* no. 17 (June, 1940); as quoted in Zabih, *The Communist Movement,* p. 116.

48. Firouz (Presentation), Paris, 30 May 1969.

49. Shayegan (Interview), New York City, 15 November 1972.

50. Interview with Nasser Khan Qasqai, the head of the Qasqai tribe, New York City, 14 September 1973.

51. *Iran-Ma,* 20 October 1946.

52. Ibid, 14 November 1946.

53. Ibid.

54. *Times,* (London), 23 November 1946.

55. *Foreign Relations of the United States,* p. 543.

56. *Khandaniha,* 24 November 1946; also Pesyan, *Death and Retreat,* pp. 231-34.

57. *Foreign Relations of the United States,* 27 November 1946, p. 548.

58. Ibid., p. 549.

59. George Lenczowski, *Russia and the West in Iran* (Ithaca, N.Y.: Cornell University Press, 1949, p. 307.

60. George Kirk, *The Middle East,* 3:80.

61. *Dad,* 4 December 1946.

62. *Foreign Relations of the United States,* 6 December 1946, p. 555.

63. George Kirk, *The Middle East,* 3:80-81.

64. Alexander Werth in the *Manchester Guardian,* 10 December 1946.

65. Pesyan, *Death and Retreat,* pp. 253-56, 223-24.

66. *New York Times,* 14 December 1946.

67. George Kirk, *The Middle East,* 3:82.

68. *New York Times,* 14 December 1946.

69. Eskandari, *Moyen-Orient* (October-November 1950 and January 1951); as quoted in Kirk, *The Middle East,* 3:82; Abdlsamad Kambakhsh, *Nazari Be Jumbesh Kargari Va Communisty Dar Iran,* [A glance at the Communist Labor Movement in Iran] (Publication of the Tudeh Party of Iran, 1972), pp. 104-5 (hereafter cited as *Communist Labor Movement*).

70. Ibid., p. 106.

71. L. P. Elwell-Sutton, *Persian Oil A Study in Power Politics* (London: Lawrence and Wishart Ltd., 1955), pp. 116-17 (hereafter cited as *Persian Oil*).

72. *Khandaniha*, 2 January 1947.

73. *Iran Ma*, 1 February 1947.

74. Ibid.

75. Komisyon-Nashr-i Vaqai-yi Siyasi, *Naft Va Bahrain* (Oil and Bahrain) (Tehran, Hassan Iqbal, 1951), pp. 9-10.

76. Ibid., p. 12.

77. Elwell-Sutton, *Persian Oil*, pp. 116-17.

78. *Keyhan*, 17 September 1947.

79. Kirk, *The Middle East*, 3:87.

80. *New York Times*, 12 September 1947.

81. Ibid.

82. *Mozakerat Majlis* [Majlis debates] (Tehran, 21 September 1947); Elwell-Sutton, *Persian Oil*, p. 118.

83. *Mozakerat Majlis* [Majlis debates] (Tehran, 5 October 1947), pp. 2159-63.

84. *Mozakerat Majlis*, [Majlis debates] 22 October 1947, pp. 2191-93.

85. Ibid., pp. 2203-4.

86. Ibid., pp. 2204-6.

87. Ibid.

88. Ibrahim Safai, *Nukhust Vaziran* [Prime ministers], (Historical Society of Iran, 1970), vol. 1, pp. 62-63.

89. Elwell-Sutton, *Persian Oil*, p. 119.

90. Safai, Nukhust Vaziran [Prime ministers] vol. 1, pp. 112-13.

91. Elwell-Sutton, *Persian Oil*, pp. 119-20.

6 The Outcome of the Azerbaijan Adventure

The purpose of this study has been to explore the dynamics of Irano-Soviet diplomacy during the 1941-47 period. However, the developments in that relationship were determined by Soviet sensitivity to British and American policy objectives in Iran. The Soviets remembered well that after World War I British troops had invaded Soviet Azerbaijan from Iran, occupying the oil center of Baku; at the same time, another British force had invaded Georgia and established headquarters in Tiflis.

Then too, there has been Lord Curzon's boast of making the Caspian Sea a "British lake," and his warnings about Russia's claims and pretensions in Iran:

> Russia regards Persia as a power that may temporarily be tolerated, that may even require sometimes to be humoured or caressed, but that in the long run is irretrievably doomed. She regards the future partition of Persia as a prospect scarcely less certain of fulfillment than the achieved partition of Poland; and she has already clearly made up her own mind as to the shore which she will require in the division of the spoils. It would be safe to assert that no Russian statesman or officer of the General Staff would pen a report upon Russian policy towards Persia and the future of that country that did not involve as a major premise the Russian annexation of the provinces of Azer-

baijan, Gilan, Mazanderan and Khorasan—in other words, of the whole of North Persia, from west to east.[1]

The establishment of security for the British empire in India, the protection of her oil concession in southern Iran, and resistance to Soviet propaganda and infiltration became the aim of British power in Iran. The pursuance of these policies led England to support the 1921 *coup d'état* in Tehran that brought Reza Khan to power. For the next twenty years the regime of Reza Shah was hostile to the Soviet Union. At first allied to Britain, the Shah later cooperated with Nazi Germany. The British used the Shah effectively to block Russian intervention in Iran before World War II.

Stalin, recalling recent history, was not ready to settle for anything less than a *cordon sanitaire* or a friendly regime on the southern border of his country. Thus, after the Soviets gained a military foothold when Anglo-Russian troops occupied Iran in 1941, Soviet authorities tried their best to create a government and a parliament friendly to Soviet aspirations.

A study of sources reveals that the refusal of the Fourteenth Majlis to accept the credentials of Pishevari and the Iranian government's secret negotiations with American oil companies both alarmed the Soviet leaders and prompted them to face Iran with their own proposals for an oil concession.

Soviet political and economic goals during this period must be examined from two perspectives. At a minimum, the Russians sought to secure the safety of their southern flank by getting an oil concession in the northern province. In effect, domination of this area would not only give them access to the agricultural and mineral resources of the richest and most fertile part of Iran, but would also establish a buffer zone between the Soviet Union and the southern and central parts of the country. The British were predominant in these areas, and the United States had just started to strengthen its position there. The maximum Soviet objective was to use the northern region as a springboard for the establishment of a Communist government in Tehran. In an interview Dr. Nouri Azadi emphasized the latter strategy. He stated that "if the Azerbaijan rebellion had lasted, it would have been a tremendous base for an attack against the reactionary regime of Iran and the conniving Shah."[2]

The initial Soviet move was to wage a diplomatic offensive to force the government of Iran to negotiate on the proposed oil concession—even while the Allies were still occupying the country. They sent an Assistant Commissar for Foreign Affairs to Tehran to dramatize that goal.

The Iranian government's response to the Russian demands was to inform all parties that there would be no concessions during the war. Furthermore, the minutes of the Iranian parliament disclosed that Dr. Mohammed Mussadeq, the leader of the nationalist alliance, gave forceful direction to the deputies of the Fourteenth Majlis in defying all foreign pressure. His heroic efforts led the Majlis to pass the Mussadeq resolution prohibiting all governments from entering into oil negotiations while Iran was under foreign occupation.

The change of attitude by the Iranian hierarchy, with double standards and secret maneuvers first in regard to the American oil companies and then to the demands of the Soviet Union, led the Russians to shift from peaceful tactics and mobilize the revolutionary phase of their campaign.

The Soviets had little difficulty in organizing the dissatisfied elements of Azerbaijan and using them to strengthen the newly formed Democratic party headed by Pishevari. Behind a Soviet screen, the "Democrats" organized their armed insurrection with the declared aim of securing autonomy in the northern provinces. This support for Pishevari proved to be a great disappointment to the nationalist forces, who had hoped that after the war the Soviet Union would act as a positive force in counterbalancing British power in Iran.

The Azerbaijan movement caused great alarm in the

nation, particularly when Pishevari's regime severed relations with the central government with the help of Russian troops. Soviet strategy was now to use the Pishevari movement as a pressure point to force an oil concession from the Iranian government. However, the Soviets erred in overestimating the strength of Pishevari's supporters. In addition, they were effectively outmaneuvered by Prime Minister Qavam, who cited the Mussadeq resolution to remind the Soviet government that there could be no agreement for an oil concession until all foreign troops were withdrawn from Iranian soil.

In later negotiations Qavam signed a draft agreement with Ambassador Sadchikov in which the Soviet Union pledged to evacuate Iran in exchange for an oil concession operated by a joint Irano-Soviet company. Qavam cleverly subjected the Iranian commitment to ultimate approval by the Fifteenth Majlis only after elections had been held and legislative activity commenced. But elections were to take place only after the withdrawal of the Red Army. The prime minister gave the Russians the impression that he had enough political power to effect election to the Majlis of members of his own party who would then ratify the accord.

The Soviets were therefore given a vested interest in paving the way for general elections across the nation, including the rebellious Azerbaijan. It had become imperative for the Soviet government to revise its policy of direct support for the Azerbaijan revolution in order to achieve an accommodation with Premier Qavam. The Soviet revolutionary adventure therefore assumed a pragmatic character, and on 9 May 1946 Russian troops withdrew from Iran.

The evidence also shows that the continued occupation of northern Iran by Soviet troops was leading to a confrontation between the United States and the Soviet Union. The Americans were demonstrating their readiness for a showdown with the Russians, and Stalin was now dealing with a powerful United States possessing the atomic bomb. The

Soviet Union was weak both economically and militarily, and was in no position to challenge the United States. In fact, Soviet national interest dictated the protection of the Russian position in Eastern Europe rather than a confrontation with the United States on another front.

While Soviet pressure and leaders of the Azerbaijan rebellion were expected to force Qavam to grant the negotiated oil agreement, Stalin hoped that by withdrawing his troops from Iran he could successfully avoid a serious break with President Truman, who had effectively exhibited his toughness in his decision to twice drop the atomic bomb on Japan.

A survey of documents indicates that even after Soviet withdrawal the United States continued its pressure. The American government effectively used its power at the United Nations to assist Iran in her case against the Soviet Union. Also of considerable importance were the actions of George V. Allen, American ambassador to Iran. He energetically supported Iranian determination to resist the Soviets. With his backing, and with pressure from the Shah, the Qavam government moved troops into Azerbaijan. The revolutionary regime collapsed after light resistance, and once again the whole nation was under the control of the central government.

The sudden downfall of Pishevari dealt a major blow to the Soviet diplomatic offensive in Iran, since the survival of his government had been a major factor in the Russian strategy. The Soviet leadership had assumed that the Azerbaijan "Democrats" would be strong enough to protect their revolution after the evacuation of Russian troops, as was the case in North Korea.

The Azerbaijan leadership was weak and inexperienced. They were unsuccessful in the area of political socialization which, according to Gabriel Almond, "is the process of induction into the political culture. Its end product is a set of attitudes—cognitions, value standards, and feelings—toward the political system, its various roles, and role incumbents. It also includes knowledge of, values affecting, and feelings towards the inputs of demands and claims into the system, and its authoritative outputs."[3]

The leaders of the Azerbaijan rebellion did not adequately communicate to the masses either the failings and the incompetence of the central government or the advantages of their own program. They also knew little about and tended to underrate the influence of the Islamic tradition and clergy over the poverty-stricken population. As a result, the peasants were not well mobilized, and the working class was neither class-conscious nor cohesive enough to lead a mass revolution.

Initially, there were strong indications that the movement's land distribution program was well supported. However, as negotiations with the central government for a peaceful solution to the insurrection continued it became necessary for Pishevari to adopt more moderate policies—especially in the area of land distribution. This led to a growing dissatisfaction amongst the peasants. In regard to the impact of other domestic measures on popular support for the regime, it should be noted that the Azerbaijan government did not last long enough to provide a concrete test for success in implementing its program.

Moreover, as this research shows, the Azerbaijan government lacked popular support because in the eyes of the people it was too dependent on foreign influence. Not only did it have to rely upon the support of Soviet authorities politically, but the Azerbaijan army was Russian-equipped and its soldiers wore Russian uniforms. In the final stages, the relationship with the Soviets became a marriage of convenience which neither side cherished. The Soviets were unhappy with the pace of the Azerbaijan revolution and its weak, inexperienced leadership. The authorities in Azerbaijan were irked by Moscow, since they felt that the Soviets were more interested in an oil concession than in the aims and aspirations of their revolution.

The demise of Pishevari strengthened the position of the Shah and his army. Candidates from Qavam's party won most of the seats in the elections for the Majlis, yet the Fifteenth Majlis not only refused to accept the oil proposal but, in short order, dropped Premier Qavam.

Finally, in understanding the Azerbaijan tragedy it is necessary to reiterate the role played by Iranian statesmen, such as Mussadeq and Qavam, in deflecting Russian incursions by means of their wily political and diplomatic maneuvers. The widsom, dedication, and patriotic devotion of these men and others laboring under impossible internal and international conditions, neutralized the foreign powers and preserved Iran's territorial integrity and national sovereignty. This achievement becomes still more remarkable with the realization that Iran not only forced the withdrawal of the occupying Red Army, but did so without becoming Communist or even allowing the Soviet Union to establish a foothold in the country.

Notes

1. George N. Curzon, *Persia and the Persian Question*, (New York: Barnes and Noble, 1966), vol. 2, pp. 593-94. Lord Curzon had gone on to claim on p. 597: "Russia's appetite for territorial aggrandisement does not stop here. Not content with a spoil that would rob Persia at one sweep of the entire northern half of her dominions, she turns a longing eye southwards, and yearns for an outlet upon the Persian Gulf and the Indian Ocean."

2. Interview with Dr. Nouri Azadi (pseudonym), member of the Central Committee of the Tudeh party, Europe, August 1973.

3. Gabriel A. Almond and James S. Coleman, eds., *The Politics of the Developing Areas* (Princeton: Princeton University Press, 1960), pp. 27-28.

Epilogue

The fall of Qavam led to several years of weak governments and the continuation of the British exploitation of the Iranian oil resource.

Meanwhile, the Iranian people who had rejected the Soviet request for an oil concession turned their attention to the task of negotiating a new oil agreement with the British.

The Iranians charged the Anglo-Iranian Oil Company with unjust distribution of the profits. Using the data available for 1948, the Iranians argued that the company's profits amounted to $320 million, yet Iran's royalty including taxes was about $32 million. At the same time the British government received from the company more than $120 million in excess profits and corporation taxes. A sum of $70 million was deposited in the reserves. Iran had no representation on the oil company's board of directors and practically no access to its accounts.[1]

The company also practiced an active policy of discrimination and segregation. In the city of Abadan, all installations and social establishments such as hospitals, swimming pools, restaurants, movie theaters, football fields, including the company's own roads and buses, were available only to Britishers. This discrimination was heightened by a visual comparison of the favorable living conditions and amenities provided for

British and other foreign employees and the sub-standard or lack of accommodations for the Iranian workers.[2]

In 1950 the report of the International Labor Organization stated that the majority of Iranian workers lived in the older section of Abadan where usually an entire family or three and four bachelors occupied one room. Some Iranian workers lived in mudhouses, straw huts, or in the 360 tents that the company had put up as an emergency measure to accommodate many homeless workers.

For the Iranian people such conditions were not only the result of political and economic exploitation but it was also a national humiliation and they were no longer willing to accept oppression disguised as a contract.

Nationalization of the Oil Industry

Late in 1947 Iran proposed to the Anglo-Iranian Oil Company a fifty-fifty profit-sharing formula similar to the one that the American companies had negotiated with Venezuela. They also demanded an extensive employment of Iranians in management, the construction of elementary and high schools in the oil fields, and the building of hospitals and apartment houses for the Iranian workers and office employees.[3]

From the beginning the company refused to discuss the profit-sharing system established in Venezuela. Furthermore, the Iranian government was told that it was impossible for the Anglo-Iranian Oil Company to accept Iran as a partner with a voice in the management of the company.

After long and bitter negotiations, the oil company came to terms with Iran on the basis of a supplementary agreement. The company reportedly agreed to provide Iran with fifty percent of the profits.

The Iranian government had to present the agreement to the Majlis for ratification. But the company had delayed too long and the attitude of the Iranian public was hostile. To the

Iranians the offer was too little and it did not guarantee an end to the company's interference in the nation's internal affairs.[4]

In the newly elected Sixteenth Majlis the opposition to the agreement was led by the National Front—headed by Dr. Mohammed Mussadeq—and a campaign was started for the nationalization of the oil industry.

On 26 June 1950 General Ali Razmara was appointed Prime Minister. He was considered by the British and the Americans as the "strong man" who could force the oil agreement through the Majlis. Razmara knew that it would be difficult to force the bill through the Majlis so he adopted delaying tactics. He ignored the numerous requests by the company to press on with the ratification of the bill.[5]

On 12 December the Majlis Oil Commission, also headed by Dr. Mussadeq, started a study of nationalization and asked Razmara to withdraw the supplementary agreement on the grounds that anything short of nationalization of the oil industry would be detrimental to Iranian Interests.[6] Premier Razmara first resisted the oil commission but eventually had to accept the advice of his majority in the Majlis that there was no possibility for the passage of the agreement. As a result Razmara withdrew the bill. The open support that Razmara gave the company discredited him in the public eye and he was accused by the press of being a "British stooge."

On 7 March 1951 Prime Minister Razmara was assassinated. With his death resistance to Dr. Mussadeq and the National Front collapsed. The cause of nationalization was taken up with fervor. In the days that followed, while the conservative royalist Hussein Ala was prime minister, a bill calling for nationalization of the oil industry was approved by the Majlis.[7] The nationalization resolution was very simple. It charged the government with the responsibility of carrying out all operations of exploration, extraction, and development of oil throughout the country.[8]

On 30 April 1951 the Majlis unanimously asked Mussadeq

to head a new government and with overwhelming popular support Mussadeq proceeded to implement the nationalization act.

The British had made the mistake of treating the oil dispute in commercial terms, believing that the demands for nationalization were staged by the Iranian negotiators in a clever move to strengthen their hand. For Iran the dispute was not that simple. For the Iranian people the conflict with the British was a national revolution against foreign exploitation and domination. Their goal was to destroy the British ability to interfere in Iranian political and economic affairs through the oil company. Moreover, Dr. Mussadeq had become the national hero of that cause and Mussadeq well understood that any settlement with the British must once and for all end the possibility of such intervention.

Throughout the period of futile oil negotiations, Premier Mussadeq successfully resisted all pressures including the complaint filed by England against Iran with the United Nations Security Council.

In the summer of 1952 Mussadeq defended Iran against the British complaint brought before the International Court of Justice. Dr. Mussadeq argued the World Court had no jurisdiction since nationalization was purely an internal act. On 22 July 1952 the International Court of Justice, adopting the Iranian viewpoint, decided it was without jurisdiction in the oil dispute. The decision greatly strengthened Mussadeq's position and he had scored another victory in his chain of many triumphs.

On 18 October 1952 the Iranians enjoyed the ultimate satisfaction when a note, addressed by the Minister of Foreign Affairs, Dr. Hussein Fatemi, to the British Charge d'affaires in Tehran, informed the British of the decision of the Iranian government to sever diplomatic relations with Britain.[9]

The *Times* of London blamed the British government for their failure in Iran. It stated that "yet it cannot be said that even in the past year British foreign policy has seemed fully to understand the character of the dispute with which it had to deal. Dr. Mussadeq, though he used his country's economic grievances against Britain to the full, and exaggerated them without scruple, has throughout been impelled by political motives unconnected with economics. His purpose is to make Persia 'neutral' in the conflicts of world powers by excluding foreign influence from his country."[10]

The Overthrow of Mussadeq

Ever since the severance of diplomatic relations and the departure of the last British employees of the oil company from the Iranian soil, the British realized that as long as Mussadeq was in power any English hope of reinstating their power over Iranian oil and Iran would be impossible. Mussadeq's government had to be overthrown. But his was the first national government since 1921 that enjoyed the support of the Iranian people. Mussadeq had fought hard to uphold the constitution by forcing the Shah to reign rather than to rule and it was a government devoid of tyranny and corruption.

The British tactics were first to undermine the power of Mussadeq by driving a wedge between his followers and to give support to any conspiracy headed by the Shah, and second to convince the Americans that Mussadeq's overthrow would be to the advantage of the western oil consumers.

As long as President Harry Truman was in the White House, he effectively resisted such pressures and insisted that the oil dispute should be settled through peaceful negotiations. He even dispatched Averell Harriman to Iran as his special envoy. Harriman was to discuss the issues with the Iranian government and make recommendations for a just solution to the dispute. However, the British government's arrogance, intransigence, and maneuvers frustrated every effort of the Truman administration.

In January 1953 Dwight Eisenhower became the President.

The British were delighted as the Eisenhower administration became their strong ally and they obtained active collaboration for their policies from Allen and John Foster Dulles. In fact, the Dulles brothers, as senior partners in the law firm of Sullivan and Cromwell, had for years represented the Anglo-Iranian Oil Company.

As the Secretary of State John Foster Dulles began supporting the British contention that if Iran were to succeed with its nationalization program this could set a precedent for other oil producing countries in the Middle East, thus endangering American interests in the area. He also accused Mussadeq of being pro-Communist.

Therefore, CIA head Allen W. Dulles was given the task of organizing the conspiracy for the overthrow of the Mussadeq government. The Shah was used as a pawn in that plot.

At first an attempt was made to destabilize the government. An Anglo-American oil boycott was instituted, circumventing the conclusion of contracts between American oil companies and Iran. The United States refused financial aid to Mussadeq and Iranian assets were frozen in London and Washington.

Next, Allen Dulles gave support to the Shah's sister Ashraf and General Fazlollah Zahedi for the recruitment and organization of the internal opposition to Mussadeq. Zahedi organized a group of retired officers, who in collaboration with the Shah actively planned the ouster of the Mussadeq government.

On 21 April 1953 under the auspices of the Shah and with the help of Zahedi's associates, General Mohammed Afshartus, Mussadeq's effective and loyal police chief, was kidnapped and tortured to death. Dr. Mussadeq's countermeasures were within the framework of the laws and the constitution, which was not an effective way of countering the terror that was beginning to operate.

In the Majlis, the opposition through absences and disruptions paralyzed the legislative process. The situation became so drastic that the majority of the deputies resigned and asked Mussadeq to submit to referendum, the termination of the Seventeenth Majlis, and the authorization for new elections.

While Premier Mussadeq was occupied with the internal opposition, economic problems, and foreign boycotts, the CIA consolidated its plan for the *coup d'état*. The evidence on the role of the CIA is best summarized by the following account:

There is no doubt at all that the CIA organized and directed the 1953 coup that overthrew Premier Mohammed Mussadegh and kept Shah Mohammed Reza Pahlavi on his throne. But few Americans know that the coup that toppled the government of Iran was led by a CIA agent who was the grandson of President Theodore Roosevelt.

Kermit 'Kim' Roosevelt, also a seventh cousin of President Roosevelt, is still known as 'Mr. Iran' around the CIA for his spectacular operation in Teheran more than a decade ago. He later left the CIA and joined the Gulf Oil Corporation as 'government relations' director in its Washington office. Gulf named him a vice-president in 1960.

General Fazollah (sic) Zahedi, the man the CIA chose to replace Mussadegh, was also a character worthy of spy fiction. A six-foot-two, handsome ladies' man, he fought the Bolsheviks, was captured by the Kurds, and, in 1942, was kidnapped by the British, who suspected him of Nazi intrigues. . .

The British and American governments had together decided to mount an operation to overthrow Mussadegh. The CIA's estimate was that it would succeed because the conditions were right; in a showdown the people of Iran would be loyal to the Shah. The task of running the operation went to Kim Roosevelt, then the CIA's top operator in the Middle East.

. . .Roosevelt operated outside of the protection of the American Embassy. He did have the help of about five

Americans, including some of the CIA men stationed in the embassy.

In addition, there were seven local agents, including two top Iranian intelligence operatives. These two men communicated with Roosevelt through cutout-intermediaries—and he never saw them during the entire operation.

As the plan for revolt was hatched, Brigadier General H. Norman Schwarzkopf, who used to appear on radio's 'Gang Busters,' turned up in Teheran. He had reorganized the Shah's police force there in the 1940s. He was best known for his investigation of the Lindbergh baby kidnapping case when he headed the New Jersey State Police in 1932. Schwarzkopf, an old friend of Zahedi's claimed he was in town 'just to see old friends again.' But he was part of the operation.[11]

On 10 August 1953 Allen Dulles packed his bags and flew to Switzerland to join his wife for a vacation. Loy Henderson, the American Ambassador to Iran, after conferring with Norman Schwarzkopf felt he could leave his post and also go to Switzerland for a short vacation. Ashraf, the Shah's sister, chose the same week to fly to a Swiss alpine resort. The secret police chief, the Ambassador, and the Iranian Princess met secretly and agreed to put into action the plan for the overthrow of Mussadeq.

Developments started to unfold: On 13 August, in the initial attempt, the Shah gave the order for the dismissal of Premier Mussadeq and the appointment of General Zahedi Prime Minister. Early in the morning of 16 August the commander of the imperial guard, Colonel Namatollah Nassiri, and officers and soldiers of the guard arrested Foreign Minister Dr. Hussein Fatemi and other governmental officials. Premier Mussadeq was to receive the same treatment but when they arrived at his residence, the Colonel and the soldiers were disarmed and arrested by government troops. The *coup d'état* failed miserably. The Shah and his wife fled to Rome by way of Iraq.[12]

The American Ambassador Loy Henderson returned to Tehran from Switzerland. Demonstrations and manifestation of support for Mussadeq took place throughout the country and for two days the people celebrated. Pictures of the Shah were removed from government offices, cinemas, and shops. Statues of his father were destroyed.

From his hiding place on 19 August Kermit Roosevelt gave the orders to his Iranian agents for the counterattack. Groups began to form in the slums of south Tehran and they merged into a shouting pro-Shah mob that marched into the heart of Tehran. The demonstrators were a strange group of *chaqu keshan* (knife wielders), weight lifters, wrestlers, gymnasts, and prostitutes. This group was similar to other chaqu keshan mobs who were usually persuaded by the money of reactionary and royalist politicians. In this case they were paid for by the Zahedi clique with CIA dollars.

It is reported that the CIA spent a total of $19 million in Iran to engineer the fall of Mussadeq. Dollars suddenly became the official currency of Tehran. Bus and taxi drivers, who transported the pro-Shah yelling mob to the various scenes of action, proudly displayed their dollar bills.[13]

Upon signal, General Zahedi, joined by some army and police units and a coalition of retired and active right wing officers, began their attack. By evening Tehran was in their hands. Zahedi became the Prime Minister and the remainder of the country accepted the new government. Mussadeq's house was looted. He and members of his government were arrested and the Shah returned to Iran.

Interestingly, the Soviet Union and the Tudeh communist party did not give Mussadeq alternate support. In fact, on many occasions, the Tudeh party press had attacked Mussadeq and during the Anglo-American oil boycott the Soviet government had turned a cold shoulder to Iran's economic problems. There were also numerous clashes between Mussadeq supporters and Tudeh demonstrators.

One wonders how different this history might have been

had the Khrushchev foreign policy been in effect during the Mussadeq years.

The Shah's Authoritarian Rule

The *coup* of 19 August 1953 (or as the Iranians call it 28 Mordad) will long be remembered as the date when the forces of imperialism and reaction triumphed over the sovereign rights of a weak Third World nation.

After the Shah's return, he immediately received all the financial and military support he wanted from the United States. The initial $45 million arrived in Iran as early as 15 September 1953, to be followed by another $15.5 million a few months later. American aid totalled $127.3 million for the fiscal year 1954.[14]

In August 1954 an international consortium of western oil companies signed a twenty-five year pact with Iran for its oil. Under it, the former Anglo-Iranian Oil Company received forty percent of the shares, a group of American Companies* obtained forty percent, Royal Dutch Shell gained fourteen percent, and the Compagnie Francaise des Petroles six percent. Iran was to receive fifty percent of the profits from the sale of oil by the consortium. Ango-Iranian was assured a compensation payment of $70 million.

Meanwhile, the Shah had used the army and the security forces to establish his authoritarian control. Ruthless purges were carried out in every stratum of society. In short a reign of terror was unleashed. Taking advantage of the situation, Zahedi submitted the oil accord to the Majlis and on 28 October the deputies, terrified and servile, quickly ratified the agreement.

The reaction of the people was one of contempt for the Shah. In their eyes he had lost his legitimacy when he fled the

* Standard Oil Company of New Jersey, Standard Oil of California, Texas Company (Texaco), Socony-Mobil Oil, and Gulf Oil Corporation.

country and was now considered a foreign agent and a man who was restored on the throne by the CIA.

To the populace the Shah was a coward, conspirator, and traitor, who was responsible for the downfall of Mussadeq's national government and the suppression of the forces who were struggling against foreign tutelage and oppression.

The United States gave additional support to the royal dictatorship when the CIA assisted in the organization, training, and arming of SAVAK (the security and information agency). It eventually became the Shah's equivalent of the Gestapo.

Lacking the ability to attract any significant popular support the Shah was compelled to rely on the instruments of terror under his control. SAVAK was used to murder, rob, torture, and destroy many individuals and families.

The horror of the SAVAK's jails and treatment of political prisoners was vividly described by Richard Savin in the International Herald Tribune of 25 November 1978. Savin, a licensed British arms salesman, was arrested in 1976 for smuggling hashish, a charge he says was a frame-up. He spent thirty months in Vakilabad prison in eastern Iran. Here is part of his report:

> Vakilabad houses 350 political prisoners. A typical case was that of Mohammed, an academic arrested by the Iranian secret police, SAVAK, for possession of two Marxist pamphlets.
>
> Hoping to extract information from him about other dissidents, SAVAK subjected him to daily beatings and tortures, including electric shocks to the temples and genitals, red hot needles under the nails, and a favorite of the jail, the 'hot-egg tango', so-called because it makes you thrash about quite a bit. The treatment consists of forcing a scalding hard-boiled egg up a prisoner's rectum. It slowly cooks your insides. Also popular was anal rape with riot sticks.
>
> The Shah's claims that no tortures or beatings go on in his jails are complete rubbish. It is also totally untrue that

thousands of political prisoners have been pardoned. Maybe one or two were let free at Vakilabad, but no more.*

Savin added that international teams investigating the treatment of prisoners were often shown Iranian army troops dressed as prisoners for the occasion.

During the long years of the Shah's personal dictatorship the Iranian economy was destroyed. The runaway inflation caused tremendous hardships for the people. There was a chronic shortage of housing and the cost of food, clothing, and rent rose beyond the means of the population. Iran, which was exporting food and raw materials to the Soviet Union and Western Europe in 1953, was importing fifty percent of its staples.

The Shah, his relatives, his cabinet, Majlis deputies, senior army officers, and high governmental officials became the center of national corruption. No significant development project was ever initiated without the involvement of the above group.

In a November 1978 speech, the Shah apologized to the Iranian people for "past mistakes, illegalities, cruelty, and corruption." He also announced that there was to be an inquiry into royal family's sources of wealth and property. To further appease the populace, the Shah ordered many of his close associates arrested on charges of corruption and abuse of power. Among them was former Prime Minister Amir Abbas Hoveida and former Chief of SAVAK General Namatollah Nassiri. Hundreds of others fled the country to avoid arrest.

The abuses of the Shah's reign were so numerous that the final result was to unite all sections of the population. Landless peasants, industrial workers, merchants of the bazaars, professionals, students, and intellectuals answered the call for revolutionary action.

Ayatollah Ruhollah al-Musavi al-Khomeini, an influential

---

*For additional information about imprisonment, torture, murder, and execution in the Shah's Iran, see *Annual Report*, Amnesty International, beginning in 1974–75, and the reports of the International Red Cross.

Shi'a religious leader who had opposed the Shah's dictatorship since the early 1960's became the rallying point of the revolution. Khomeini had been imprisoned several times by SAVAK and in 1964, on the orders of the Shah, was exiled to Iraq. Ayatollah Khomeini's main aim was to overthrow the despotic monarchy and to replace it with an Islamic republic.

The revolutionaries achieved their goals mainly by non-violent means. The tactics employed against the Shah's powerful forces were the use of a network of Mullahs (clerics), in order to organize secret cells throughout the country and to promote the political consciousness of the masses. The Mullahs and their operatives distributed underground newspapers, circulars, and cassettes bearing messages from exiled Ayatollah Khomeini. Added to these activities were mass demonstrations and industrial strikes, especially in the oil fields.

The Shah's government confronted the opposition by resorting to brutal force. The army and SAVAK agents shot indiscriminately at the demonstrators using automatic weapons, tanks, and helicopter gunships. Thousands were killed and injured. Despite the heavy casualties the people continued their massive demonstrations and on 16 January 1979 the Shah was forced to leave Iran.

The armed forces that the Shah had turned into his personal body guards by lavishing upon them an enormous quantity of money and sophisticated weapons, were plagued by a corrupt, ineffective, self-serving senior officer corps. On 11 February, after two days of fighting against the revolutionary forces, they became totally demoralized and collapsed.

Under the leadership of Ayatollah Khomeini the Pahlavi dynasty was abolished and the populace, voting in a nation-wide referendum, approved the establishment of an Islamic Republic. In addition, having learned well the lessons of the Mussadeq experience the Ayatollah moved quickly to uproot and destroy all of the power centers of the old regime.

This book is a mirror reflecting the hopes, desires, dreams, frustrations, sacrifices, and struggles of the masses in pursuit of freedom from internal tyranny and external domination. Indeed, after thirty-seven years of struggle, much bloodshed and destruction, having achieved total victory over the forces of oppression, it becomes imperative for the revolutionary leadership to commence the task of building a new Iran and satisfying the long desired needs of the people.

Notes

1. Nasrollah Saifpour Fatemi, *Oil Diplomacy: Powderkeg in Iran* (New York: Whittier Books, Inc., 1954), pp. 329-30 (hereafter cited as *Oil Diplomacy*).

2. Bahman Nirumand, *Iran the New Imperialism in Action* (New York: Monthly Review Press, 1969), p. 46 (hereafter cited as *Iran the New Imperialism*).

3. Ibid.

4. Keyhan, 20 April 1951.

5. Hussein Makki, *Kitab-i Siah* (The Black Book) (Tehran, 1950), pp. 332-40.

6. Ibid.

7. Richard W. Cottam, *Nationalism in Iran* (Pittsburgh: University of Pittsburgh Press, 1967), p. 205 (hereafter cited as *Nationalism in Iran*).

8. Fatemi, *Oil Diplomacy*, p. 339

9. Cottam, *Nationalism in Iran, pp. 219-20*.

10. *Times* (London), 29 October 1952.

11. David Wise, and Thomas B. Ross, *The Invisible Government* (New York: Bantam Books, 1965), pp. 116-19.

12. *Nirumand, Iran the New Imperialism*, pp. 85-86.

13. Ibid., p. 87.

14. Ibid., p. 93.

Appendixes

Appendix A

Excerpts from the Treaty of Friendship between Iran and
the Russian Socialist Federal Soviet Republic,
signed at Moscow, 26 February 1921

ARTICLE 1

In order to confirm its declarations regarding Russian policy
towards the Persian nation, which formed the subject of corres-
pondence on the 14th January, 1918, and the 26th June, 1919, the
R.S.F.S.R. formally affirms once again that it definitely renounces
the tyrannical policy carried out by the colonising Governments of
Russia which have been overthrown by the will of the workers and
peasants of Russia.

Inspired by this principle, and desiring that the Persian people
should be happy and independent and should be able to dispose
freely of its patrimony, the Russian Republic declares the whole
body of treaties and conventions concluded with Persia by the
Tsarist Government, which crushed the rights of the Persian
people, to be null and void.

ARTICLE 2

The R.S.F.S.R. expresses its reprobation of the policy of the
Tsarist Governments of Russia, which, on the pretext of ensuring
the independence of the peoples of Asia, concluded, without the
consent of the latter, treaties with European Powers, the sole object
of which was to subjugate those peoples.

This criminal policy, which infringed upon the independence of the countries of Asia and which made the living nations of the East a prey to the cupidity and the tyranny of European robbers, is abandoned unconditionally by Federal Russia.

Federal Russia, therefore, in accordance with the principles laid down in Articles 1 and 4 of this Treaty, declares its refusal to participate in any action which might destroy or weaken Persian sovereignty. It regards as null and void the whole body of treaties and conventions concluded by the former Russian Government with third parties in respect of Persia or to the detriment of that country.

ARTICLE 3

The two Contracting Powers agree to accept and respect the Russo-Persian frontiers, as drawn by the Frontier Commission in 1881.

At the same time, in view of the repugnance which the Russian Federal Government feels to enjoying the fruit of the policy of usurpation of the Tsarist Government, it renounces all claim to the Achouradeh Islands and to the other islands on the Astrabad Littoral, and restores to Persia the village of Firouzeh and the adjacent land ceded to Russia in virtue of the Convention of the 28th May, 1893.

The Persian Government agrees for its part that the Russian Sarakhs, or "old" Sarakhs, and the land adjacent to the Sarakhs River, shall be retained by Russia.

The two High Contracting Parties shall have equal rights of usage over the Atrak River and the other frontier rivers and waterways. In order finally to solve the question of the waterways and all disputes concerning frontiers or territories, a Commission, composed of Russian and Persian representatives shall be appointed.

ARTICLE 4

In consideration of the fact that each nation has the right to determine freely its political destiny, each of the two Contracting Parties formally expresses its desire to abstain from any intervention in the internal affairs of the other.

ARTICLE 5

The two High Contracting Parties undertake:
(1) To prohibit the formation or presence within their respective

territories, of any organization or groups of persons, irrespective of the name by which they are known, whose object is to engage in acts of hostility against Persia or Russia, or against the Allies of Russia. They will likewise prohibit the formation of troops or armies within their respective territories with the aforementioned object.

(2) Not to allow a third party or organization, whatever it be called, which is hostile to the other Contracting Party, to import or to convey in transit across their countries material which can be used against the other party.

(3) To prevent by all means in their power the presence within their territories or within the territories of their Allies of all armies or forces of a third party in cases in which the presence of such forces would be regarded as a menace to the frontiers, interests or safety of the other Contracting Party.

ARTICLE 6

If a third party should attempt to carry out a policy of usurpation by means of armed intervention in Persia, or if such Power should desire to use Persian territory as a base of operations against Russia, or if a Foreign Power should threaten the frontiers of Federal Russia or those of its Allies, and if the Persian Government should not be able to put a sotp to such menace after having been once called upon to do so by Russia, Russia shall have the right to advance her troops into the Persian interior for the purpose of carrying out the military operations necessary for its defense. Russia undertakes, however, to withdraw her troops from Persian territory as soon as the danger has been removed.

ARTICLE 7

The considerations set forth in Article 6 have equal weight in the matter of the security of the Caspian Sea. The two High Contracting Parties therefore have agreed that Federal Russia shall have the right to require the Persian Government to send away foreign subjects, in the event of their taking advantage of their engagement in the Persian navy to undertake hostile action against Russia.

Appendix B

Treaty of Alliance between the United Kingdom and the
Soviet Union and Iran,
signed at Tehran, 29 January 1942

His Majesty The King of Great Britain, Ireland, and the British
Dominions beyond the Seas, Emperor of India, and the Union of
Soviet Socialist Republics, on the one hand, and His Imperial
Majesty The Shahinshah of Iran, on the other;

Having in view the principles of the Atlantic Charter jointly
agreed upon and announced to the world by the President of the
United States of America and the Prime Minister of the United
Kingdom on the 14th August, 1941, and endorsed by the Government of the Union of Soviet Socialist Republics on the 24th
September, 1941, with which His Imperial Majesty The Shahinshah declares his complete agreement and from which he wishes
to benefit on an equal basis with other nations of the world; and

Being anxious to strengthen the bonds of friendship and mutual
understanding between them; and

Considering that these objects will best be achieved by the
conclusion of a Treaty of Alliance;

Have agreed to conclude a treaty for this purpose and have appointed as their plenipotentiaries;

His Majesty The King of Great Britain, Ireland and the British
Dominions beyond the Seas, Emperor of India,

For the United Kingdom of Great Britain and Northern Ireland,
His Excellency Sir Reader William Bullard, K.C.M.G.,
C.I.E.,
His Majesty's Envoy Extraordinary and Minister
Plenipotentiary in Iran.

The Union of Soviet Socialist Republics,
> His Excellency M. Andre Andreewich Smirnov, Ambassador
> Extraordinary and Minister Plenipotentiary of the
> Union of Soviet Socialist Republics in Iran.

His Imperial Majesty The Shahinshah of Iran,
> His Excellency M. Ali Soheily, Minister for Foreign
> Affairs.

Who, having communicated their full powers, found in good and due form, have agreed as follows:

ARTICLE 1

His Majesty The King of Great Britain, Ireland and the British Dominions beyond the Seas, Emperor of India, and the Union of Soviet Socialist Republics (hereinafter referred to as the Allied Powers) jointly and severally undertake to respect the territorial integrity, sovereignty and political independence of Iran.

ARTICLE 2

An alliance is established between the Allied Powers on the one hand and His Imperial Majesty The Shahinshah of Iran on the other.

ARTICLE 3

(i) The Allied Powers jointly and severally undertake to defend Iran by all means at their command from all aggression on the party of Germany of any other Power.

(ii) His Imperial Majesty The Shahinshah undertakes—

(a) to co-operate with the Allied Powers with all the means at his command and in every way possible, in order that they may be able to fulfil the above undertaking. The assistance of the Iranian forces shall, however, be limited to the maintenance of internal security on Iranian territory;

(b) to secure to the Allied Powers, for the passage of troops or supplies from one Allied Power to the other or for other similar purposes, the unrestricted right to use, maintain, guard and, in case of military necessity, control in any way that they may require all means of communication throughout Iran, including railways, roads, rivers, aerodromes, ports, pipelines, and telephone, telegraph and wireless installations;

(c) to furnish all possible assistance and facilities in obtaining material and recruiting labour for the purpose of the maintenance and improvement of the means of communication referred to in paragraph (b);

(d) to establish and maintain, in collaboration with the Allied Powers, such measures of censorship control as they may require for all the means of communication referred to in paragraph (b).

(iii) It is clearly understood that in the application of paragraph (ii) (b), (c) and (d) of the present article the Allied Powers will give full consideration to the essential needs of Iran.

ARTICLE 4

(i) The Allied Powers may maintain in Iranian territory land, sea and air forces in such number as they consider necessary. The location of such forces shall be decided in agreement with the Iranian Government so long as the strategic situation allows. All questions concerning the relations between the forces of the Allied Powers and the Iranian authorities shall be settled so far as possible in co-operation with the Iranian authorities in such a way as to safeguard the security of said forces. It is understood that the presence of these forces on Iranian territory does not constitute a military occupation and will disturb as little as possible the administration and the security forces of Iran, the economic life of the country, the normal movements of the population and the application of Iranian laws and regulations.

(ii) A separate agreement or agreements shall be concluded as soon as possible after the entry into force of the present Treaty regarding any financial obligations to be borne by the Allied Powers under the provisions of the present article and of paragraphs (ii) (b), (c) and (d) of Article 3 above in such matters as local purchases, the hiring of buildings and plant, the employment of labour, transport charges, etc. A special agreement shall be concluded between the Allied Governments and the Iranian Government defining the conditions for any transfers to the Iranian Government after the war of buildings and other improvements effected by the Allied Powers on Iranian territory. These agreements shall also settle the immunities to be enjoyed by the forces of the Allied Powers in Iran.

ARTICLE 5

The forces of the Allied Powers shall be withdrawn from Iranian territory not later than six months after all hostilities between the Allied Powers and Germany and her associates have been suspended by the conclusion of an armistice or armistices, or on the conclusion of peace between them, whichever date is the earlier. The expression "associates" of Germany means all other Powers which have engaged or may in the future engage in hostilities against either of the Allied Powers.'

ARTICLE 6

(i) The Allied Powers undertake in their relations with foreign countries not to adopt an attitude which is prejudicial to the territorial integrity, sovereignty or political independence of Iran, nor to conclude treaties inconsistent with the provisions of the present Treaty. They undertake to consult the Government of His Imperial Majesty The Shahinshah in all matters affecting the direct interests of Iran.

(ii) His Imperial Majesty The Shahinshah undertakes not to adopt in his relations with foreign countries an attitude which is inconsistent with the alliance, nor to conclude treaties inconsistent with the provisions of the present Treaty.

ARTICLE 7

The Allied Powers jointly undertake to use their best endeavors to safeguard the economic existence of the Iranian people against the privations and difficulties arising as a result of the present war. On the entry into force of the present Treaty, discussions shall be opened between the Government of Iran and the Governments of the Allied Powers as to the best possible methods of carrying out the above undertaking.

ARTICLE 8

The provisions of the present Treaty are equally binding as bilateral obligations between His Imperial Majesty The Shahinshah and each of the two other High Contracting Parties.

ARTICLE 9

The present Treaty shall come into force on signature and shall remain in force until the date fixed for the withdrawal of the forces of the Allied Power from Iranian territory in accordance with Article 5.

In witness whereof, the above-named plenipotentiaries have signed the present Treaty and have affixed thereto their seals.

Done at Teheran in triplicate in English, Russian and Persian, all being equally authentic, on the 29th day of January, 1942.

(L.S.)　R. W. Bullard
(L.S.)　A. A. Smirnov
(L.S.)　Ali Soheily

Appendix C

The Anglo-American-Soviet Declaration Concerning Iran, issued at Teheran, 1 December 1943

The President of the United States of America, the Premier of the U.S.S.R., and the Prime Minister of the United Kingdom, having consulted with each other and with the Prime Minister of Iran, desire to declare the mutual agreement of their three Governments regarding relations with Iran.

The Governments of the United States of America, the U.S.S.R. and the United Kingdom recognize the assistance which Iran has given in the prosecution of the war against the common enemy, particularly by facilitating the transportation of supplies from overseas to the Soviet Union. The three Governments realize that the war has caused special economic difficulties for Iran and they agreed that they will continue to make available to the Iran Government such economic assistance as may be possible, having regard to the heavy demands made upon them by their world-wide military operations and to the world-wide shortage of transport, raw materials and supplies for civilian consumption.

With respect to the post-war period, the Governments of the United States of America, the U.S.S.R. and the United Kingdom are in accord with the Government of Iran that any economic problem confronting Iran at the close of hostilities should receive full consideration along with those of other members of the United Nations by conferences or international agencies, held or created, to deal with international economic matters.

The Governments of the United States of America, the U.S.S.R. and the United Kingdom are at one with the Government of Iran in their desire for the maintenance of the independence, sovereignty and territorial integrity of Iran. They count upon the participation of Iran, together with all other peace-loving nations, in the establishment of international peace, security and prosperity after the war, in accordance with the principles of the Atlantic Charter, to which all four Governments have continued to subscribe.

APPENDIX D

The Iranian Constitution
30 December 1906

ARTICLE 24

The conclusion of treaties and agreements and the concessions of commercial, industrial, agricultural or other monopolies must be authorized by the National Assembly. Treaties which it may be in the interest of the government or nation to keep secret are excepted.

Selected Bibliography

Almond, Gabriel A., and Colman, James S., eds. *The Politics of the Developing Areas.* Princeton: Princeton University Press, 1960.

Amidi-Nuri. *Azerbaijan-i Demukrat* [The Azerbaijan Democrats]. Tehran: 1946.

Amuzgar, Hussein. *Naft Va Havades Azerbaijan* [Oil and the events in Azerbaijan]. Tehran: November 1947.

Arfa, Hassan. *Under Five Shahs.* New York: William Morrow and Co., 1965.

Bahar, M. *Tarikh-e Mokhtasar-e Ahzab-e Siyasiye Iran* [A short history of the political parties of Iran]. Tehran: Sherkat-e Sahami Chap, 1944.

Banani, Amin. *The Modernization of Iran, 1921-1941.* Stanford: Stanford University Press, 1961.

Beloff, Max. *The Foreign Policy of Soviet Russia.* Vol. 2, London: Oxford University Press, 1952.

British Broadcasting Corporations. *Daily Digest of Foreign Broadcasts,* no. 769. 26 August 1941.

Byrnes, James F. *Speaking Frankly.* New York: Harper and Brothers, 1947.

Churchill, Winston S. *The Grand Alliance, The Second World War.* Boston: Houghton Mifflin Company, 1950.

Cotton, Richard W. *Nationalism in Iran.* Pittsburgh: University of Pittsburgh Press, 1967.

Curzon, George N. *Persia and the Persian Question.* Vol. 2. New York: Barnes and Noble, 1966.

Department of State. *Foreign Relations of the United States, The Near East and Africa, 1946.* Vol. 3. Washington: U.S. Government Printing Office, 1969.

Eagleton, William. *The Kurdish Republic of 1946*. London: Oxford University Press, 1963.

Elwell-Sutton, L. P. *Persian Oil: A Study in Power Politics.* London: Lawrence and Wishart Ltd., 1955.

――――. "Political Parties in Iran, 1941-1948." *Middle East Journal*, vol. 3, no. 1, 1949.

Erani, Taghi. *Bashar as Nazare Maddi* [Man from a materialistic viewpoint]. Tehran: 1945.

Eskandari, Iraj. "Histoire de Partie Tudeh." *Moyen-Orient*, no. 6, December 1949.

Fatemi, Nasrollah Saifpour, *Oil Diplomacy: Powderkeg in Iran.* New York: Whittier Books, Inc., 1954.

Garagani, Manshur. *Siasate Dowlate Showravi Dar Iran as 1296-1306* [The policy of the Soviet government in Iran from 1917-1929]. Tehran: Chapkhaneh Mozaheri.

Grant, Christina Phelps. "Iran: Test of Relations between Great and Small Nations." *Foreign Policy Report*, vol. 21, no. 3, 15 April 1945.

Homayounpour, Parvis. *L'affaire d'Azerbaidjan*. Lausanne: 1965.

Hurewitz, J. D. *Diplomacy in the Near and Middle East.* Princeton: D. Van Nostrand Company, Inc., 1956.

――――. *Middle East Dilemmas*. New York: Harper and Brothers, 1953.

――――. *Middle East Politics: The Military Dimension*. New York: Praeger Publishers, 1970.

Iran, *Qanun-e Assassi* [Iran, the constitution]. Tehran: Majlis Press.

Jacobs, Norman. *The Sociology of Development, Iran as an Asia Case Study*. New York: Frederick A. Praeger, 1966.

Kambakhsh, Abdlsamad. *Nazari Be Jumbesh Kargari Va Communist Dar Iran* [A glance at the Communist labor movement in Iran]. Publication of Tudeh Party of Iran, 1972.

――――. "Nazari Betarikh Hezab Tudeh Iran" [A look at the history of the Tudeh party of Iran.] *Donya*, vol. 7, no. 1, Spring 1957.

――――. "Tashkil Hezab Tudeh Iran" [The structure of the Tudeh party of Iran]. *Donya*, vol. 7, no. 3, Autumn 1957.

Kirk, George. *The Middle East in the War, Survey of International Affairs, 1939-1946*. Vol. 2. London: Oxford University Press, 1952.

————. *The Middle East, Survey of International Affairs, 1945-1950.* Vol. 3. London: Oxford University Press, 1954.

Komisyon-Nashr-i Vagai-Yi Siyasi. *Naft Va Bahrain* [Oil and Bahrain]. Tehran: 1951.

Lambton, Ann K. S. *Landlord and Peasants in Persia.* London: Oxford University Press, 1953.

Lederer, Ivo J., ed. *Russian Foreign Policy.* New Haven: Yale University Press, 1962.

Lenczowski, George. *Russia and the West in Iran.* Ithaca, N.Y.: Cornell University Press, 1949.

Lenin, V. I. *Sochinennia* 19:22.

————. *Sochinennia* 19:220-22; as quoted in Eudin, Xeina J., and North, Robert C., *Soviet Russia and the East, 1920-1927.* Stanford: University Press, 1957.

Makki, Hussein. *Kitab-i Siah* (The Black Book). Tehran: 1950.

————. *Tarrikh-e Bist Salleh Iran* [Twenty years history of Iran]. Vol. 2. Tehran: Majlis Press, 1946.

————. Vol. 3. 1947.

Mashkur, Mohammed Javad. *Nazari Beh Tarikh-e Azerbaijan Va Asar Bastani Va Jmayyat Shenasi-An* [Reflection on the history of Azerbaijan and its ancient heritage and demographic characteristics]. Tehran: The National Heritage Society of Iran, 1969.

Massudi, Qassem. *Jarayan Mossaferat Mission Azemie Iran be Moscow* [An account of the Iranian mission to Moscow]. Tehran: Printing Association, Inc., 1947.

Menken, Jules. "Britain and the Persian Question." *The National Review,* vol. 126, January 1949.

Millspaugh, Arthur C. *American in Persia.* Washington: The Brookings Institutions, 1946.

Ministry of Foreign Affairs. *Official Journal of Iran,* no. 238. Tehran: 5 December 1945.

Ministry of Labor and Propaganda. *Iran dar Rah Eslahat Democratic* [Iran at the threshold of Democratic reforms]. Tehran, 1946.

Mozakerat Majlis [Majlis debates]. Tehran: 12 December 1925; 12 August 1944; 19 October 1944; 2 December 1944; 3 December 1944; 18 April 1945; 20 October 1945; 29 November 1945; 18 December 1945; 7 January 1946; 29 February 1946; 21 September 1947; 5 October 1947; 22 October 1947.

Nirumand, Bahman. *Iran the New Imperialism in Action.* New York: Monthly Review Press, 1969.

Nouri, Ebrahim Khajeh. *Bazigaran-e-Asr-e Talaie, Soheili* (The actors of the golden age, Soheili). Tehran: Adalat Newspaper Publications, 1320/1941.

Official Publication of the Government of Iran. *Evolution of Communism from Shahrwar 1320* [September 1941] *to Farvardin 1336* [April 1957]. Tehran: 1959.

Ostovan, Hussein Kay. *Siasat-i-Movazeneh-i- Manfiey Dar Majlis Chardahom* (Establishment of a negative equilibrium in the Fourteenth Majlis). Vol. 1. Tehran: Majlis Publishing Press, 1949.

———. Siasat-i-Mavazeneh-i-Manfiey Dar Majlis Chardaham (Establishment of a negative equilibrium in the Fourteenth Mjlis). Vol. 2. Tehran: Tabin Press, 1951.

Peaslee, Amos J. *Constitution of Nations.* Concord: The Rumford Press, 1950.

Pesyan, Najafgoli. *Marg Bud Bazgast Ham Bud* [There were both death and retreat]. Tehran: 1944.

Radmanesh, Reza. "Dar Bareh Nahzat 21 Azar" [About the 21st of Azar movement]. *Donya*, vol. 6, no. 4, Winter 1959.

Rossow, Robert Jr. "The Battle of Azerbaijan 1946." *Middle East Journal*, Winter 1959.

Safai, Ebrahim. *Nukhust Vaziran* [Prime ministers]. Vol. 1. Tehran: Historical Society of Iran, 1970.

Sontag, R. J., and Beddi, J. S., eds. *Nazi-Soviet Relations, 1939- 1941: Documents from the Archives of the German Foreign Office.* New York: Didder, 1948.

Spector, Ivar. *The Soviet Union and the Muslim World.* Seattle: University of Washington Press, 1959.

Stettinius, Edward, Jr. *Roosevelt and the Russians, The Yalta Conference.* New York: Doubleday and Co., Inc., 1949.

Truman, Harry S. *Truman Speaks.* New York: Columbia University Press, 1960.

United Nations. *Official Records of the Security Council.* 1st Year, 1st Series, No. 1.

———. *Official Records of the Security Council.* 1st Year, 1st Series, No. 2.

United States. *Department of State Bulletin.* 17 March 1946.

———. *Department of State Bulletin.* 7 April 1946.

Upton, James. *History of Modern Iran: and Interpretation.* Cambridge: Harvard University Press, 1960.

Wilbur, Donald N. *Iran Past and Present.* Princeton: University Press, 1963.

Wise, David, and Ross, Thomas B. *The Invisible Government.* New York: Bantam Books, 1965.

Zabih, Sephr. *The Communists Movement in Iran.* Berkeley: University of California Press, 1966.

Iranian Periodicals

Adalat

Eqdam

Bakhtar

Dad

Donya

Ettelaat

Iran Ma

Keyhan

Khandaniha

Mehr-Iran

Paykar

Qeyam Iran

Rahbar

Setareh

Index